VENETIAN GLASS

THE NANCY OLNICK AND GIORGIO SPANU COLLECTION

Foreword by Nancy Olnick and Giorgio Spanu

Introduction by Holly Hotchner

Essays by: David Revere McFadden, Marino Barovier, Suzanne K. Frantz

Photographs by Luca Vignelli

Book Design by Massimo Vignelli

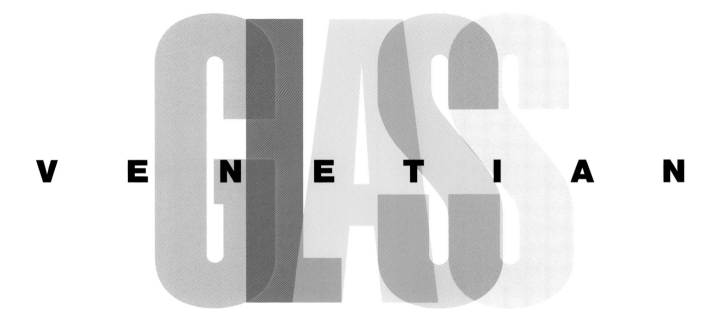

Venetian Glass: 20th Century Italian Glass
The Nancy Olnick and Giorgio Spanu Collection
The American Craft Museum
Exhibition held in New York, Fall 2000
Museum Curator: David Revere McFadden
Guest Curator: Marino Barovier
Exhibition Design: Massimo and Lella Vignelli with David Law
Catalogue Research and Historical Documentation edited by: Marino Barovier
English Edition edited by: Susan Sacks
Technical Advisor: Howard J. Lockwood
Graphic Production: Piera Brunetta

Support for this publication has been received from Furthermore, the
publication program of The J.M. Kaplan Fund, and the Italian Cultural Institute.

Museum Edition ISBN 1-890385-05-0
The American Craft Museum, New York

Trade Edition ISBN 88-8158-296-1
Edizioni Charta, s.r.l. Milano

Library of Congress Card Number: 00-106478

Worldwide distribution by Edizioni Charta s.r.l.
Via della Moscova, 27
20121 Milano, Italy
Telephone +39 02 6598098 Fax +39 02 6598200

USA distribution by D.A.P Distributed Art Publishers, Inc.
155 Sixth Avenue, 2nd floor
New York, NY 10013, USA
Telephone 212 627 1999 Fax 212 627 9484

Printed and bound by Tipografia Rumor S.p.a.
Via Dell'Economia, 127
36100 Vicenza, Italy
Telephone +39 0444 961566 Fax +39 0444 963311

First Edition, July 2000

Contents

Nancy Olnick and Giorgio Spanu   *Foreword, 6*

Holly Hotchner   *Introduction, 8*

David Revere McFadden   *Remembering the Future: Collectors and Collecting of Venetian Glass, 10*

Marino Barovier   *The Art of Muranese Glass, 13*

Suzanne K. Frantz   *Not One Without The Other: The Collaboration Between Artist and Craftsman in Muranese Glass, 20*

Artist Statements   *Alfredo Barbini, 22*

Cristiano Bianchin, 22

Laura Diaz de Santillana, 24

Benjamin Moore, 24

Yoichi Ohira, 25

Tobia Scarpa, 25

Thomas Stearns, 26

Lino Tagliapietra, 27

Massimo Vignelli, 28

Toots Zynsky, 28

Nancy Olnick and Giorgio Spanu   *The Collection, 32*

Marino Barovier   *Catalogue of the glass, 202*

Artists, 236

Vetrerie (Workshops), 244

Glossary, 246

Bibliography, 248

Foreword
Nancy Olnick and Giorgio Spanu

Little did Giorgio and I realize what we were getting ourselves into when we impulsively—now looking back, instinctively—acquired our first piece of Murano glass. We went to an auction house to pick up a contemporary art catalogue and decided to take a look at the current exhibition of decorative arts. From across the room, a half-cobalt blue, half-emerald green hourglass caught my attention. We loved it and left a bid. We didn't think about the piece again until the auction house phoned to inform us that our bid had been successful.

The minute I placed the piece next to our *Flowers* painting by Andy Warhol, it was magic. I don't know whether it was the light or the juxtaposition of 1950s Italian glass and 1960s American Pop Art, but the combination worked. Our passion for Murano glass had begun. In a short time we acquired many wonderful pieces from local fairs, galleries, and auctions around America.

However, we wanted to study, to educate ourselves. It was difficult because there was a dearth of literature available on Murano glass. On one of our trips to Italy, Giorgio noticed a two-line ad in *In Flight* magazine regarding a glass exhibition titled *Art of the Barovier*. Though it was not on our itinerary, we went to Venice for a day to see what turned out to be a magnificent collection of 20th century Murano glasswork. Mesmerized by the design and craftsmanship, we were determined to meet the curator, Marina Barovier.

As luck would have it, she was in Venice and we arranged a meeting. Our education had begun.

Initially, and understandably, it was the colors that attracted us, as well as the unusual shapes from the 1950s. Fulvio Bianconi's sensual forms and colorful patchwork designs were impossible to resist. Dino Martens's African-inspired *Oriente* and *Eldorado* series were some of the most exciting pieces of glass we'd ever seen. Archimede Seguso's *Merletti* had an ethereal elegance. We were hooked.

We decided to go back to the beginning of the 20th century. We discovered Vittorio Zecchin, Artisti Barovier and Napoleone Martinuzzi, who were beginning to break away from the over-elaborate forms and dense colors of 19th century Venetian glass in favor of a more restrained style, transparent glass, and intricate mosaic techniques. The time had come when chandeliers, glasses and vases started to be recognized as works of art. Murano was gaining worldwide recognition at the hands of these masters.

As we continued our journey, we were very fortunate to meet knowledgeable, generous people who guided us from piece to piece. Perhaps some of our most prized pieces are those of Thomas Stearns, one of the first Americans ever to have glass works produced by the Venini factory. Although he spent a short period in Murano, from the end of 1959 to the end of 1962, his designs were amazingly complex and innovative. As we discovered more about glass, we began to gravitate to the years between 1925 and 1945. There was one designer in particular who took our breath away, the Venetian architectural genius, Carlo Scarpa. The simplicity of his forms, his Eastern influences, and his novel glassmaking techniques brought a modernism to Murano that it had never before seen. His work became the ultimate focus of our collection. To us, each of his pieces is a jewel.

Our collection takes us to Murano at least once a year. We find it fascinating to watch this art in the making. The *maestri* blow glass today in the same way as they did 700 years ago; we are continually amazed by the inexplicable form of communication that takes place between the designer and the glassblower. Today, we are watching the development of Cristiano Bianchin, Yoichi Ohira, Laura Diaz de Santillana and Lino Tagliapietra. While the individual sensibilities of these artists vary, they are all creating works in the time-honored tradition of Murano.

Interestingly enough, after all our education and experience, we collect glass today in much the same way we did when we were drawn to our first piece. We rely on instinct. We are attracted to some forms because of their simplicity. Others may be more complex, but it is their color that captivates us. We can be drawn to an intricate technique. Inevitably, we react to the synergy of the piece. We particularly like vases. Perhaps it is their grace and fragility coupled with the idea that they are, at the same time, usable vessels. We love the way the glass itself reflects light and enhances its immediate surroundings. These art forms have a magical presence—something you can't really grasp all at once, or even explain—although you can pick a piece up and hold it in your hand. And when you do hold it in your hand, it vibrates with its own life. This is the moment in which we decide whether or not to purchase a piece of glass.

Giorgio and I have been very fortunate to have discovered the world of Murano. Searching for glass has been an educational experience for us. Even more than that, living among these pieces has decorated our day-to-day lives with flashes of color and light and joyful inspiration.

We are so pleased to have our collection on view at the American Craft Museum. The Museum's dedication to Craft and Design makes it the ideal environment for us to share our love of Venetian glass. We especially want to thank Holly Hotchner for her enthusiasm and support of this project. A special note of thanks to David Revere McFadden for his essay concerning the historical perspective on collections in this field. We thank Suzanne Frantz for her insights into the complex relationship between designer and *maestro*. We were particularly touched by the immediate responses of the following glass artists who thoughtfully shared their memories, feelings and experiences of working in Murano and the world of glass: Alfredo Barbini, Cristiano Bianchin,

Laura Diaz de Santillana, Benjamin Moore, Yochi Ohira, Tobia Scarpa, Thomas Stearns, Lino Taliapietra and Toots Zynsky. Our collaboration with Lella and Massimo Vignelli has been nothing short of inspiring. Their love of glass and brilliant design sense has elevated this project to unimagined heights and, as the adage says, "The apple does not fall far from the tree." Luca Vignelli has created the finest glass photographs we have ever seen. His dedication to perfection is clearly manifested in his patience and passion for his work. We are most grateful to Marino Barovier, who has contributed his archives, material, and extensive knowledge to the making of this book. Murano glass has been part of his family's legacy to the world and we are deeply appreciative that he has shared it with us.

We would like to offer our thanks to Carlo Rumor for the elegant printing of this book. We thank Piera Brunetta for painstakingly preparing the mechanicals over and over again. A very special thanks to David Law for his talent and vision in the design of this exhibition.

Many thanks to Susan Sacks for struggling with all the translations to ensure they remained true to the intent of the author and to Howard Lockwood for perfecting the english translation of the bibliography and the descriptions of each piece.
Their help was invaluable.

Our deepest gratitude to our dear friend and associate, Albert Ayache, for his tireless devotion and dedication.

Finally, a note of love to our children Eve, Robert, and Stella, who immediately jumped into this exciting adventure with us and participated in the selection and placement of our collection: and also, for never breaking a single piece!

Introduction
Holly Hotchner, *Director American Craft Museum*

Glass as a medium for creative expression has been in the forefront of the mission of the American Craft Museum since its founding 44 years ago. In its inaugural years, the Museum mounted one of the first major exhibitions in the United States dedicated to Louis Comfort Tiffany. Tiffany, in addition to being recognized as America's greatest genius in glass, was also an entrepreneur who transformed the great European traditions of glassmaking into a distinctly American art form.

Glass is a unique material with its own special technical history. The past four decades have seen fantastic creativity in the field of glass, particularly a trajectory launched with the studio glass movement of the 60s. Artists working in this media continue to challenge its physical and creative boundaries.

American glass today has been dramatically shaped by the great glass tradition of Venice. Early on, in 1964, the Museum recognized the importance of Italian glass by organizing an exhibition on Italian and Czech glass. This current exhibition and publication give a comprehensive overview of the 20th century Italian glass tradition, which will contextualize American glass within the international world. After all, it is within the context of the great Italian glassmakers coming to this country to work and teach—as well as, to a limited degree, seeing objects through publications and exhibitions—that American glass as an art form developed.

Italian glass was unique in that it eroded the boundaries between fine and decorative arts and design. Architects, painters, sculptors and artisans were attracted to the field, which became a virtual melting pot for many artistic forms of expression. With this exhibition and publication, the Italian glass centers and creators are documented and presented.

This extraordinary collection is the result of the vision of Nancy Olnick and Giorgio Spanu, who have created a collection that has no equivalent in private or public hands. The objects have been discovered, acquired and researched over the past ten years through sheer passion and tenacity. Despite the scarcity of published or exhibited material, the Spanus have diligently educated themselves in the techniques and makers of Italian glass from the turn of the century until today. Through their unique "treasure hunt," both Nancy and Giorgio have become outstanding connoisseurs in this field. The collection is continuing to grow through their active involvement with artists working today. It is the museum's great privilege to be enriched by their knowledge, vision and generosity and we will watch their collection continue to grow with keen interest.

The Spanus have been aided by the great knowledge of—and dedication to—Italian glass by Marino Barovier. Related to the great glass manufacturer bearing his name, Marino has painstakingly documented the history of the glass centers in Italy in the 20th century. As importantly, he has identified the artists and forms produced in these factories during specific years. The museum is indebted to his years of work and is privileged to be able to publish this chronology and history.

Both the exhibition and publication design have been realized through the creative genius of Massimo and Lella Vignelli. Through their firsthand experience of creating and designing glass, they have developed a unique vision of how to display and experience these glass objects. As a result, the objects are brought to life through a seemingly effortless environment of light. The publication has also given the opportunity for the first collaboration of the Vignellis with their son the talented photographer Luca, who also brings the deep appreciation and understanding of glass to his extraordinary photographs. The museum and its public is indebted to the Vignellis for the extraordinary experience of viewing these objects.

The project has been expertly guided by David McFadden, the museum's chief curator and vice president of exhibitions and programs. David's deep understanding of the history of glass in all of its forms has added immeasurably to this project and his essay gives new insights into the impact of Italian glass on the development of glass in America.

Remembering the Future:
Collectors and Collecting of Venetian Glass

David Revere McFadden, *Chief Curator American Craft Museum*

"History is a pattern of timeless moments," wrote poet T. S. Eliot. In the history of the decorative arts, timeless moments are captured by objects that have been conceived, made, possessed, preserved, and cherished. Artists and collectors are linked by objects that serve as the tangible records of creation and collection.

For well over five centuries, glass from Murano has been an object of desire for collectors of all persuasions, ranging from royalty to day-trip tourists. The extraordinary skill of the glassmakers of Murano, magicians able to transform a mute material into the poetry of light and color, has been recorded over the centuries in vases, sculptures, chandeliers, and elegant drinking glasses. Glass from Murano has come to symbolize the cultural history of an island and its unique artisanal culture.

If history is a pattern of timeless moments, it is also an ambivalent force. The writer G. K. Chesterton compared history to a hill that offered a vantage point from which we may see clearly the age in which we are living. For others, like the industrialist Henry Ford, history kept creative minds in chains (*"the only history that is worth a tinker's damn is the history we make today."*)

For artists, history can be a great and dependable ally, but it can also hamper innovation and new ideas. Artists, like inventors, writers, politicians, and theologians, have struggled with history in different ways: by reasserting the traditional values of materials, techniques, and familiar designs, or by challenging the seductive reassurance of history through experimentation, creative innovation, and new ideas. The popularity of Italian glass over hundreds of years, and its special popularity in the 19th century as a commodity for the ever-increasing number of tourists who visited Venice, encouraged the growth of the industry, but also dictated that historical styles reflecting the virtusoso traditions of Venice were faithfully copied. As the growing number of tourists transformed a floating village into a major theme park, tradition reasserted itself with a vengeance. Collectors sought out traditional Venetian glass objects and trinkets—beautifully handcrafted using centuries-old techniques of blowing and lampwork. The economics of popular taste maintained high standards of technical excellence in Murano right through the 19th century and even to the present day. Such fidelity to tradition, however, also stifled creativity among a new generation of artists, architects, designers, and entrepreneurs, who sought to bring the art of the glassmaker into the 20th century, and to respond to the new world of visual, spatial, and intellectual ideas it represented.

Embracing the best of the past while rebelling against suffocation is not an easy challenge. Strains of new artistic ideas that were percolating in Europe in the closing years of the 19th century also encouraged experimentations in glass. Innovative and non-traditional works created in Venice shortly after 1900 were in a new style, inspired by nature-based floral designs created by European artists, or by stylized decorations derived from Japanese models. The new style in Italy, fresh and antihistorical in appearance, is most often referred to as *stile Liberty*. Glass made in this new style was often decorated with tapestry-like floral patterns inlaid into simple vase forms, primarily for a discerning and elite clientele by firms such as the legendary Barovier. While the other "popular" glasshouses of Murano continued to flood the market with mind-boggling and complex chandeliers and tableware that faithfully reproduced the colors and designs of the 18th and 19th centuries, a new spirit of innovation and change could be detected in these early modern works.

The experiments and innovations of the early 20th century set the stage for a dramatic series of changes that would take Italian glass from the realm of historical decorative arts to the world of radical modern design.

Some of the innovations in early modern Italian glass were the result of contact with designers from other parts of Europe. As early as 1914, Hans Stoltemberg Lerche (1867-1920) from Scandinavia, designed vases in a new, modern, heavy-walled style at the Toso factory. These were shown at the 1914 Biennial as well as at the 1920 Biennial and the famed International Exhibition of Decorative Arts at Monza in 1923. Our knowledge of early modernist Italian glass within its larger critical context is based on a scant number of such examples and, in most cases, such innovations were overshadowed in the popular sphere by the power of tradition that kept Italian glass within its 19th century historical mode.

Collectors of the "new" or "modern" style of Venetian glass were in short supply, something other brave artists and manufacturers, such as Paolo Venini, were to learn. The primary outlet for showing works in the new style were major international exhibitions, most notably the Paris 1925 exhibition in which both Italian and Swedish glass were praised for their quality and significance to the developing modern movement in design. And while sophisticated American collectors and some curators traveled to such exhibitions and fairs to acquire selected pieces in the new mode, few pieces of Italian glass made between World Wars I and II were exported for sale into the United States. Rare exceptions included the adventurous selection of a *fazzoletto* vase by Fulvio Bianconi by the Museum of Modern Art in New York in 1949.

It was the growth of a secondary market spurred by museum exhibitions, adventurous galleries and dealers and, to a lesser degree, by the auction houses, that brought 20th century Italian glass into the mainstream. For the average consumer, Venetian glass as promoted in magazines such as Arts & Decoration in the 1930s saw few examples of truly innovative glass in a new style—most were reproductions or replicas of famous works. While occasional articles featured simple modern shapes in *filigrana* glass from M.V.M Cappellin (Arts & Decoration, May 1932), most coverage in the popular press looked backwards to history as the true source of Venetian genius in the field of art glass. For example, Eugene Wright in "A Twentieth-Century Renaissance of Venetian Glass," in Arts & Decoration for May 1939, extolls that *"it is only of recent years that this goal [of achieving world supremacy in the crystal art] has been reached, and that one has been able to speak in the same breath of Venice-Murano goblets and the creations of her great Barovier of the 15th Century."*

It was not until after the second World War that Venetian glass established a beachhead in America, often in company with Scandinavian glass from Sweden and Finland, countries that could also boast of skilled artisanal traditions that survived the war and which required modest economic investment to grow. From the 1950s forward, the profile of Venetian glass in America began to change, as wider segments of the public were able to view the works of major contemporary creators and glasshouses in shops, museum exhibitions, and in a growing number of illustrated books. International knowledge of Venetian glass was enhanced by publications such as Domus, which took the lead in promoting Italian design industries, architects and designers, and manufacturers, and the growing number of design exhibitions being organized in major European cities after the war.

The famed Milan Triennale was reinstated in 1947, highlighting award-winning work by modern designers, and prestigious design awards, such as the *Compasso d'Oro* sponsored by La Rinascente department store. Such awards lent glamor to the promotion and advertising of consumer goods and aided in the economic development of the industry.

For Americans, probably the most important single event was the creation of an extraordinary exhibition in 1950, titled *Italy at Work: Her Renaissance in Design Today*, organized by the curator of decorative arts and industrial arts at the Art Institute of Chicago, Meyric Rogers. The catalogue for the exhibition featured a foreword by the illustrious American designer Walter Dorwin Teague, and was published in Italy by the Compagnia Nazionale Artigiana, the national organization to promote craft and design.

What made *Italy at Work* so important was not just the selection of the objects, which ranged from traditional and non-traditional woodworking and ceramics to innovative enamels, metalwork and, especially glass, but the broad exposure it brought for Italian design. The exhibition traveled to major city museums in Baltimore, Buffalo, Chicago, Houston, Minneapolis, Brooklyn, Pittsburgh, Portland ME, Providence RI, San Francisco, and Toledo. Walter Dorwin Teague acknowledged the important truce that had been forged by Italian designers with their own persuasive cultural history when he noted in his foreword that *"Barbini's art, modern as its forms are, has descended to him from his forefathers of Murano."* Teague goes on to repeat the legend, however, that Barbini's forefathers *"fought off invading Venetians with balls of hot glass on the ends of their blowpipes."*

Rogers set the stage for this new Italian renaissance by noting that *"No visitor to Italy within the last two or three years can have failed to be impressed by two things, first by the extent of the war's destruction and second by the extraordinary rapidity with which it is being repaired. Only slightly less obvious is the accompanying surge of creative activity in other fields."* With great foresight, Rogers also noted that a defining characteristic of the new modern designs emanating from Italy was its disregard for traditional categorization that separated art, craft, and design into separate fields: *"The romantic snobbism which draws a qualitative distinction between the fine and applied arts has little prevalence in Italy. Here the earlier pre-academic tradition still exists that sees nothing eccentric in an artist working in any or all of these forms of expression as occasion arises."*

The list of glass artists and firms included in the exhibition reads like a Who's Who of Murano glass: in addition to firms from Milan, Florence, Empoli, and Naples, the Venetian contingent was comprised of Barovier & Toso, Alfredo Barbini, Nason & Moretti, Flavio Poli, Giuseppe Torres, Seguso, and Paolo Venini.

The ramifications of this kind of publicity were notable. By the mid-1950s, more and more articles began to appear that highlighted truly modern glass from Venice. For example, *Craft Horizons* magazine featured Italian modern glass in its March-April 1955 issue, as well as a January-February 1956 article focusing on the new designs being created in Murano by American Charles Lyn Tissot, one of the first Americans to participate directly in the making of glass in Murano. Important exhibitions of Italian modern glass were held in Europe, such as that shown at the Musée des Arts Decoratifs in Paris in 1956 and another devoted to the work of Venini and Orrefors held in Hannover in 1957. Venini, always in the vanguard of effective marketing, sponsored a number of exhibitions of the factory's works in both Europe and the United States, but there was little available information about or exposure for the other designers and firms. In 1959, the Corning Museum of Art's landmark *Glass 1959; a special exhibition of international contemporary glass*, which traveled to the Art Institute of Chicago, New York's Metropolitan Museum of Art, the Toledo Museum of Art, and the Virginia Museum of Fine Arts in Richmond, also highlighted work by Barovier & Toso, such as their famous "basket-weave" vessels, six pieces by Flavio Poli, ten from Venini, and others by Archimede Seguso, Dino Martens, and Carlo Nason, among others.

In America, the spheres of interest for a growing number of collectors of earlier 20th century design in the 1960s and 70s (mostly Art Nouveau and Art Deco) did not extend frequently to Italian glass, in spite of surprisingly avant garde exhibitions such as that held at the Museum of Contemporary Craft (now the American Craft Museum) in 1964 titled *Glass: Czechoslovakia/Italy*. For dedicated or emerging collectors interested in acquiring examples of major work by leading designers, regular trips to flea markets and estate auctions were necessary.

While the literature on Venetian glass continued to develop in the 1960s, 70s, and early 80s (see bibliography), it was in the 1980s that American museums began to take collectors of modern Venetian glass seriously. Important inspiration came from two different, but related sources—dealers and museums. In 1981 the Smithsonian Institution Traveling Exhibition Services organized and circulated a major overview of Venini glass. In 1983 Frances Pratt organized a small exhibition of forty pieces of glass, most from the 50s and 60s, titled *Murano Glass in the Twentieth Century* for the Museum of Fine Arts in St. Petersburg, Florida, the first effort to present an overview of Venetian glass in the United States. This was followed in 1984 by *Venini & the Murano Renaissance of the 1940s & 1950s*, an exhibition of sixty-three pieces of modern Venetian glass, organized by Fifty-50 Gallery, New York. In the catalogue, gallery co-owner Mark Isaacson wrote that Italian glass artists *"experimented endlessly with daring and original forms, used brilliant, varied, sometimes shocking colors, and brought exciting and innovative techniques to an art thousands of years old."* Important to future collectors were the short but useful histories of the major firms compiled by Eric Helton. In 1989, Muriel Karasik Gallery in New York exhibited *The Venetians: Modern Glass 1919-1990*.

By the 1990s, along with a more general growth of interest in 20th century design by a new generation of curators, scholars, collectors, and dealers, and a subsequent increase in the number of design exhibitions to feature modern Italian glass, a general collecting frenzy followed. Auction houses responded by including more and more examples of Italian glass in modernism sales, and museums across the United States began collecting and exhibiting modern Venetian glass on a larger scale than ever before.

The renaissance of interest in Italian glass in the 20th century, however, was due in great part to collectors who recognized both its quality as art and its significance as cultural document. Collectors from the 1950s forward maintained and nurtured an interest in Venetian glass that extends to the present moment. It is significant that the Olnick Spanu collection does not stop at the close of the 20th century, but continues today with work by emerging and established artists who are creating Venetian masterpieces of glass for the future. If history is about timeless moments, collecting is about timeless qualities that have made Venetian glass such a powerful medium. The present exhibition is a perfect resumé of two collectors' personal odyssey, and their graciousness in sharing their passion with the public.

The Art of Muranese Glass

Marino Barovier, *Historian*
Specializing in 20th Century and Contemporary Venetian Glass

"Murano glass needs no illustration. It is too famous all over the world; and the number of people who love its splendor and its grace is truly impressive. Is there anyone who has never heard of its lightness, its transparency, its iridescence; and those colors and shapes which appeared to a poet as the essence of Venetian beauty (….)." Stated over forty years ago in the introduction to the exhibition on Murano glass held at the Museum of the Decorative Arts in Paris in 1956, these thoughts remain relevant to this day. Despite the progress made by technology and the constant availability of new materials, the production of Murano glass, which descends from the centuries-old tradition of craftsmanship, is the object of renewed interest in our contemporary era. Completely indifferent to new technology, Murano glass is still shaped by hand using age-old handcrafting techniques. The basis of these techniques is the free blowing of molten glass. Transferred from the *crucible* to the *pontil* rod with the blower's pipe, the molten glass is gathered at the extremity of this steel hollow tube to form an incandescent mass which is then blown. The resulting irregular bubble is shaped with the use of metallic tools of various dimensions, or by using specific molds. In some cases, the molten glass is gathered by a solid pipe and shaped without being blown to obtain various sculptural forms. During the phases of blowing and shaping, the incandescent mass on the blowing pipe is repeatedly reheated in the furnace to maintain the required fluidity. Upon completion, the object is detached from the *pontil* and transferred into the *annealing* oven where it will undergo a progressive cooling process to minimize internal tensions in the glass which would cause breakage in the finished object.

The history of Venetian glass has remote origins which some authors trace back to the Roman glass tradition developed in the town of Aquileia. Others connect the budding of this art to the presence of a glass industry linked to the Benedictine monasteries founded in areas throughout the Venetian lagoon sometime around the 9th century. The intense trade carried out by the Venetian Republic with the Orient and the world of Islam, where glass technique was quite advanced—especially after the 11th century—was also influential to its development. In any case, at the end of the 10th century (982), the first written documents testify to the existence, in Venice, of *maestri fioleri*; glass workers who produced *fiole* or vials, thin-necked containers for liquids blown out of glass. During the second half of the 13th century (1271), the *fioleri* had already formed a trade association regulated by the written law Capitulare de fiolariis, later replaced by the Mariegola dei vetrai in 1441. In addition, the Serenissima Republic of Venice took a number of protectionist measures to safeguard its exclusivity of glass production. After 1291, by decree of the Maggior Consiglio (Venetian high government) to protect the city of Venice from fire hazards, all furnaces were transferred to the island of Murano where many glassmakers had already established themselves. In fact, the settlement of numerous furnaces along the canal of Santo Stefano on Murano caused its bank to be renamed fondamenta dei Verieri—today it is called dei Vetrai—which translates to "of the glassmakers".

Murano's glass industry grew steadily through the middle of the 15th century. During this time its production of blown glass was remarkable and it established a leadership position for Murano on the international market. This was due, not only to the incentives and protectionist laws decreed by the Serenissima, but also because of the extraordinary quality of the vessels, goblets, plates and decanters produced on the island. These were generally blown out of thin colored glass and often embellished with painting and decoration in golden enamels or brilliant colors. In the second half of the 15th century, Angelo Barovier, a member of one of the most renowned families of glassmakers, invented a terse clear glass with extreme transparency. It was called *cristallo* because of its similarity to rock crystal and its use soon became one of the distinct characteristics of Venetian glass.

Production during the following century was particularly refined, and its harmonious classical forms adorned many European Renaissance palaces. This was a period of great success for Murano glass as its glassmakers perfected many new techniques for the creation of unique glass textures such as *filigrana*. Despite the restrictions imposed by the Venetian Republic against the exportation of Murano glass techniques to other countries, the second half of the 16th century and the early 17th century witnessed a significant emigration of glassmakers abroad where numerous glass workshops were founded. In several European countries new factories produced glassware commonly called *façon de Venise*, manufactured in the tradition of blown glass, but gradually evolving through the benefit of local influences.

In the 17th century, the advent of the Baroque style guided Venetian glass production toward an overabundance of decoration on lightweight *soffiati* (free blown glass). The growing success of the finely cut, heavy Bohemian crystal cost Venetian glass its, until then, dominant position on the market. Consequently, at the turn of the century, a new fashion was imported—and not without difficulty—to Murano. It is here that Giuseppe Briati, during the first half of the 18th century, succeeded in producing a *cristallo*, containing potash. While it was similar to Bohemian crystal, its particular characteristics gave it a brilliance that distinguished it, making it more suitable for the engraved decoration consonant with the Baroque taste. However, in keeping with local tradition, 18th century Murano production continued with the use of singular, dominating color embellishments which characterized, for example, its famous chandeliers.

The advent of foreign competition, the stubborn hostility demonstrated by the Venetian glassmakers toward technical innovations, and the lack of openness towards what was happening in Europe, lay the groundwork for the serious crisis which hit the glass sector during those years. This crisis took a turn for the worse after the fall of the Venetian Republic in 1797. A period of depression followed which saw the growing availability of foreign glass on the local Venetian market and the progressive decline and closing of many of the Murano glass workshops.

After the 1830s and 40s, sporadic attempts to revive Venetian glass were made by many people including the antique dealer Sanquirico and glass experts Domenico Bussolin, Pietro Bigaglia and Lorenzo Radi, who either personally or indirectly dedicated their efforts to reviving ancient techniques such as *filigrana*. It was the work of the abbot Vincenzo Zanetti which proved to be largely responsible for leading Murano glass towards a decisive Renaissance. In 1861, Zanetti founded the Glass Museum of Murano for the sole purpose of opening a school of design and glass technique for craftsmen. The examples of glassworks from the past which were offered as study models gave the new *maestri* the means to reclaim techniques Murano had once been famous for but which had almost been lost over time. Sharing Zanetti's intentions was the lawyer, Antonio Salviati from Vicenza, who had already opened a large mosaic workshop in Venice in 1859. In 1866, he used English capital to found Salviati & C. for the production of light *soffiati* glass pieces. He was able to count on the best *maestri* of the island—among them Antonio and Giovanni Barovier, Antonio Seguso, Vincenzo Moretti, Andrea Rioda and others. With great foresight, he required that all of them attend Zanetti's design school. Thus, he was able to achieve a remarkable quality of production inspired by the best glass tradition of the previous centuries.

Salviati & C. was so successful that in 1867 he received numerous awards at the Universal Exposition in Paris. Ten years later, Mr. Salviati, released from his obligations to Salviati and C., left the workshop and founded Salviati dott. Antonio. He took the remarkably skilled Barovier brothers, Antonio and Giovanni, with him. They were joined, later, by Antonio's sons, Giuseppe and Benvenuto. In 1883, when Salviati decided to devote himself entirely to the selling of glass, the Barovier's acquired ownership of the company by promising to produce glass exclusively for Mr. Salviati. They changed the name of the company to Artisti Barovier after Salviati's death in 1890.

Over the last decades of the 19th century, production in Murano was prolific having achieved a newfound vigor by copying 16th, 17th and 18th century models. Unfortunately, the limitation implicit in this practice led to a style dominated by sterility which was incapable of renovating Murano glass. Once again, the island proved remarkably deaf to innovation, which in those years—especially in the field of decorative arts—was represented by the oncoming of *stile Liberty*.

At the turn of the century, the French works of Gallé, Daum and Lalique, along with Tiffany glass from America, were inspired by this new movement and were gathering growing consensus. On Murano, these influences were acquired in a sporadic manner and only after they had lost their original vitality everywhere else. Slight changes could be perceived in 1895 at the Murano glass exhibition which the island held at the same time as the first Esposizione Internazionale d'Arte di Venezia (Biennale). Artisti Barovier received awards for several modern objects among which was a goblet with a spiral stem.

By 1910, Venetian glasswork was showing more convincing evidence of innovation. This was due largely to contacts established with a number of artists, most of whom belonged to the dynamic, anti-academic atmosphere of Cà Pesaro. These artists, like Vittorio Zecchin and Teodoro Wolf Ferrari, collaborated with the Artisti Barovier and, belated though it was, began to open up a world of glass which manifested the influence of Art Nouveau. The pieces that exemplified this most were the brightly colored vessels and plates in *vetro mosaico* executed by the Artisti Barovier and the unusual glass pieces exhibited at the Biennale designed by the ceramic artist Hans Stoltemberg Lerche. The latter were created between 1912 and 1914 for Fratelli Toso, a glass workshop founded in 1854.

The onset of World War I interrupted work in the furnaces, and with it, this still occasional collaboration between artists and the glass workshop which had sprung from a curiosity on the part of the artists. Having made it through the war years, the Artisti Barovier, renamed Vetreria Artistica Barovier after 1919, proceeded with the experimentation it had conducted with Vittorio Zecchin and Teodoro Wolf Ferrari and presented several vessels made in the *vetro mosaico* technique. Despite the fine quality of the pieces, which were created by the young Ercole and Nicolò Barovier themselves, glass produced at the Vetreria Artistica Barovier continued to reflect the previous Art Nouveau orientation even though in their most abstract decorations they did reflect an interest in expressionism.

True innovation in Murano glass came largely with the *"courageous modern reform of Vittorio Zecchin, Venini and Cappellin"* (G. Lorenzetti, 1932). In 1921, the Milanese Paolo Venini and the Venetian Giacomo Cappellin founded a new furnace called V.S.M. Cappellin Venini & C. Its production, designed by the painter Vittorio Zecchin, encountered remarkable success from the very beginning and it was recognized as being truly avant-garde. In response to the request for sobriety and sophistication made by the two partners Venini and Cappellin—their reference being the cultured society of the upper middle class—Zecchin created glass pieces which abandoned all superfluous decoration. These were inspired, at times, by the Renaissance paintings of Titian and Veronese and were generally distinguished by their truly rarefied quality. Extreme thinness and the delicate colors of the transparent material distinguished the pieces executed by the skilled *maestri* of the V.S.M. Cappellin Venini. These pieces earned the glowing appreciation of Lorenzetti in his history of Murano glass, where he particularly praised their *"very simple forms in the rhythm and in the harmonious flight of their line, created to exalt the most tenuous, almost evanescent coloring, lightness and lucid transparency, the two unique gifts of Murano glass (....)"* (G. Lorenzetti, 1931). The glass workshop received considerable acclaim in many exhibitions, in particular the Biennale of Monza, founded in 1923, which soon became a reference point in the field of decorative arts.

However, in 1925, after having represented Italian craft production together with Richard Ginori at the prestigious Exposition Internationale des Arts Décoratifs et Industriels de Paris, Giacomo Cappellin and Paolo Venini ended their partnership and founded two distinct companies: Giacomo Cappellin founded Maestri Vetrai Muranesi Cappellin & C. and Paolo Venini founded Vetri Soffiati Muranesi Venini & C. Vittorio Zecchin continued to serve as the art director of Maestri Vetrai Muranesi Cappellin & C. until 1926, creating new lightweight *soffiati* with classical proportions which positioned the company as one of the best glass workshops of Murano in the 20s—even though, due to economic misfortunes, the company was to last only a very short time. Soon after Vittorio Zecchin left the furnace, the young Venetian architect Carlo Scarpa

Interior of a Muranese workshop, early 20th century.

Archimede Seguso, one of the most sophisticated interpreters of 20th century Murano glass.

Alfredo Barbini, highly skilled maestro creator of innovative techniques such as il guanto di carta bagnata *(the wet paper glove technique).*

took his place as artistic director and further developed the concepts left by his predecessor. The new production distinguished itself for its essential design, reflecting the formal simple lines Zecchin had initiated previously. Among the most significant works of Scarpa's early years is, without a doubt, the spherical vessels with a conic base, originally presented in thin clear glass. These became the logo of Maestri Vetrai Muranesi Cappellin & C. Paolo Venini also chose to involve another artist from Murano in his newfound glass workshop; a sculptor named Napoleone Martinuzzi. Martinuzzi, at the time, was the director of the Murano Glass Museum and was to become the artistic director of Vetri Soffiati Muranesi Venini & C. through 1932. This marked the first of a long series of productive collaborations which Venini, always open to innovation from the contemporary design and architectural worlds, would repeatedly conduct with artists and architects of his time. This openness would prove to be the distinctive characteristic of his workshop, to which he dedicated himself without interruption until his death in 1959. Paolo Venini contributed significantly to the vitality of 20th century glass. The debut of the new Venini glass workshop saw Napoleone Martinuzzi initially attempt to take on the heritage left by Vittorio Zecchin. At the beginning he remained faithful though he soon developed a refined series of clear glass pieces in *filigrana* (1927) which captured the attention of Giò Ponti in the first issue of Domus. *"Here are the filigrane again, particularly appreciated for their technical and manual difficulty which require a more than perfect knowledge of glass (....)"* (Domus 1928, January). Towards the end of the 20s, however, Martinuzzi began experimenting with new formulations of glass and created an opaque glass, *pulegoso*, which looked spongy and owed its peculiarity to the countless micro-bubbles which remained trapped inside the glass. Born of the necessity to keep up with the aesthetics of the time, just as interior design was converting to the squared-off *Novecento* style, this new technique served Martinuzzi well and he used it to present objects endowed with a remarkable sculptural quality.
In a short time (1930), Vetri Soffiati Muranesi Venini & C. produced a wide range of *pulegosi* designed by Napoleone Martinuzzi. These can be recognized by their soft shapes in imitation of antique amphoras and vessels, accompanied by unique *cactus* all in *pulegoso* glass, with large ones done in shades of dark green. Many of these pieces were presented in Monza in 1930 at the 4th Triennale where the question of opaque glass was widely debated. It raised bitter dissent from the critics who, in the name of Murano's tradition, upheld that glass, in order to remain glass, had to respect the criteria of lightness and transparency. *"If one must consider absolute the criterion that art must necessarily adhere to the intimate substance of its chosen material, that is, that the arts must always respect and make evident the essential and characteristic qualities of their material, then most of the glass pieces displayed at the Triennale di Monza should be repudiated."* Clearly, Carlo Alberto Felice reservedly comments on the pages of Dedalo (1930, fasc. V), *"the possibilities and resources of this fascinating material appear infinite (....) and if imitations of other materials which have been made and continue to be made with glass are not to be encouraged, they may be considered*

interesting experiments (...) as long as they do not change the nature of glass and do not betray its essential characteristics...."
On the pages of Domus, though not without some discomfort, Carlo Alberto Felice did not hide his opinion that Venini's new pieces will always remain worthy of respect. *"When they are discovered in ten years or two centuries time, it will be said, these are the pulegoso that the Venini glass workshop made around the 1930s"* (Carlo Alberto Felice, 1931).
At the close of the 20s, Scarpa, just like Martinuzzi, tended towards the use of opaque glass. *"In the latest works from Cappellin the material has been transformed. So it appears in the precious and milk-white glass pieces which (....) have once again exalted the superior virtues of our glassmakers"* (Domus, 1928, December). And again, *"Lattimi, exquisite gold and silver glass by Cappellin, (....) glass with vivid polished compact colorings (...)"* (Domus 1930, July) were repeatedly praised on the pages of the trade reviews and at the exposition in Monza. They received wider acclaim by the critics because of Felice's view that *"these works, though not akin to the classical way of understanding glass (...) don't want to be or look like anything but glass, which reveals its other hidden properties"* (Carlo Alberto Felice, 1930). And according to the Venetian Ugo Nebbia *"M.V.M. Cappellin & C. (...) reveals its own intentions, perhaps even more refined, but more traditionally akin to our own art glass"* (U. Nebbia).
Carlo Scarpa's collaboration produced many collections distinguished by the refined nature of the design and the superior quality of the glass. He chose his techniques from the many which had fallen into disuse which he reinterpreted in a strictly personal manner; for example, he enriched the thin *lattimi* by applying gold or silver leaf. The debate on opaque glass proved to be fruitful. Though it brought out a certain uneasiness on the part of critics who found themselves viewing works apparently free of the Murano glass tradition, at the same time it hinted at the greater potential of the material and suggested new directions for experimentation. In the following years, this would lead to truly extraordinary innovative creations.
In general, the Cappellin production designed by Carlo Scarpa was truly remarkable, characterized by vivid colors made possible by glassmakers working in the furnace. Sensitive to the demands of fashion, Maestri Vetrai Muranesi Cappellin & C. also created a series of sculpturally unique animals. Unfortunately, in spite of their extraordinary success, economic mismanagement forced Cappellin to close down his company in 1932.
Among the other glass workshops present in Monza in 1930, the Vetreria Artistica Barovier & C. also presented a series of pieces whose originality drew considerable interest.
But it was not just for their unusual forms, like many of the pieces exhibited in Monza. The *Primavera* glass series by Ercole Barovier proved to be fascinating for their unique glass texture, in particular, for *"the originality of the execution which consists in having brought to this art the craquelé used in porcelain. The Primavera series acquire greater beauty through this process and their slightly pearly reflections seem to capture the light with a very fine fishnet, the submarine light of some fantastic jellyfish"* (La casa bella 1930, May).

Despite the repeated success of the *Primavera* series, which were also recognized at the 1930 Biennale of Venice, the *primavera* glass could only be used to make a limited number of objects. This was due to the fact that this type of glass had been created by accident and the process could never be repeated.
When the Biennale Internazionale d'arte di Venezia finally opened to decorative arts in 1932, a new pavilion was dedicated to this art form giving it adequate exhibition space. Now the city of Venice was given another opportunity to view the latest production and the most advanced experimentation of artists working in the furnaces on Murano. Decorative arts, including glass, have not been exhibited at the Biennale Internazionale d'arte di Venezia since 1972. Napoleone Martinuzzi also participated in the opening of this new exhibition of Murano glass with brightly colored *paste vitree* as well as soberly elegant *incamiciati* pieces. After leaving Vetri Soffiati Muranesi Venini & C. in 1932, Napoleone Martinuzzi founded the Zecchin-Martinuzzi glass workshop with Francesco Zecchin.
At the same 1932 Biennale, Vetri Soffiati Muranesi Venini & C. production was highly praised *"for the re-born linear simplicity of those delicate blown pieces, turquoise and black, green and gold, and especially that most clear and aristocratic white and silver (....)"* (U. Nebbia 1932). These designs were created by the pencil of the Milanese architect Tomaso Buzzi, who was the art director of Vetri Soffiati Muranesi Venini & C. until 1933. He also designed another series of vessels in pastel-colored opaque glass obtained by the overlay of several layers of color sumptuously decorated with applications of gold leaf finished in *pasta vitrea*.
The following year the Vetri Soffiati Muranesi Venini & C. was able to boast the presence of Carlo Scarpa who remained the acting artistic director through 1947. His debut at Venini in 1934, was marked by the creation of the delicate *filigrane* series, a personal reinterpretation of the ancient Murano glass techniques. This was done by experimenting with technique after technique. In addition, in the same year, Scarpa produced the glass series *Sommersi a bollicine* whose bold tones were enhanced by the inclusion of gold leaf. Enriched by experience gained at Maestri Vetrai Muranesi Cappellin & C., Carlo Scarpa, assisted by the dedication of Paolo Venini himself (who, in some cases, personally intervened in designing), created a truly remarkable variety of pieces. These were enthusiastically received by critics and provoked a wide variety of descriptions by commentators. G. Dell'Oro speaks of *"Murano glass drowned inside raw crystal which forms a sort of colored ring, like a transparent incrustation of stalactites"* (G. Dell'Oro, 1935). On the pages of Domus the *sommersi* were described as *"vessels and bowls made with Murano glass then submerged in a clear cristallo that constitutes a sort of transparent shell around the colored center, like a nutshell"* (Domus 1934, September). The *sommersi*, which were developed into other models in 1936, were followed by the vast series of *corrosi*, which were decorated with *bugne* or *fasce applicate* and known for the thickness of their glass.
Over the following decade, Scarpa's productive experiments resulted in a wide range of glass pieces such as the thin multi-colored rods, *tessuti*, the oriental-like shaped *cinesi*, the splendid a *murrine* bowls with *battuto* surfaces and the transparent vessels decorated a *fili*, a *fasce* or a *pennellate*. These were shown at many exhibitions of

decorative arts and established Carlo Scarpa and Vetri Soffiati Muranesi Venini & C. as the true leaders of Murano glasswork of that period.

Alongside Carlo Scarpa's inventions in the 30s, Ercole Barovier, had become artistic director of Vetreria Artistica Barovier, also distinguishing himself for using very thick glass to which he gave new expression. He accomplished this with the use of the technique *colorazione a caldo senza fusione* which he himself had created. From 1934-1935, he enriched his glass pieces with single colors achieved through this new technique and from this, the *Crepuscolo*, the *Laguna Gemmata*, the *Marina Gemmata* and the *Autunno Gemmato* collections were born. All are known for their unique shades of color. At the 1936 Biennale, the Ercole Barovier glass workshop, renamed in that year Ferro Toso Barovier, presented several of *"its heavy glass pieces entitled Autunno Gemmato which, considering concept, technique and material, seem to be right on the mark and in line with current trends"* (G. Dell'Oro, 1936).

After the great success obtained by the Vetreria Artistica Barovier in the early 30s, other glass workshops such as S.A.I.A.R. Ferro Toso and Seguso Vetri d'Arte were able to establish themselves with a wide variety of pieces. The 40s witnessed a progressive decline in the activity of the smaller companies which were driven to hardship by the onslaught of the war. This was not the case with the glass workshops run by Paolo Venini or Ercole Barovier which continued to produce and present new works at the exhibitions. The comments by Domus regarding the participation of Barovier Toso & C., formerly Ferro Toso Barovier, at the 7th Triennale of Milan in 1940 appear to be significant. Barovier *"Presented with the generous mastery of his talent and his great passion.... (He shows) works of vibrant, new, free and shocking inspiration (....) it is in fact twenty years that these be-deviled Muranese are renewing themselves and creating a profitable future for Italian art glass with a liveliness, a tirelessness and an abundance which has no equal (...)"* (Domus 1940, May).

During the post-war period, and for the entire duration of the 50s, glasswork on Murano went through another truly significant period. New energy channeled through the work of many designers actively collaborating in the furnaces led to the creation of objects characterized by greater expressive freedom. It was largely thanks to the contribution of vital figures such as Flavio Poli, Dino Martens and Fulvio Bianconi that a fundamental renovation occurred.

Poli preferred shapes with an out of proportion linear quality which could be seen as vaguely Nordic and which led to the elegant *sommersi* such as the *Valva* pieces produced in 1954 by Seguso Vetri d'Arte. These pieces were extremely successful and they were awarded the prestigious Compasso d'Oro in 1954. In the early 50s, Dino Martens, reinterpreting the traditional techniques of Murano in an original manner, created for the Aureliano Toso workshop glass pieces with variegated colorful textures obtained from specific rods of *zanfirico,* with which he made his *Zanfirici, Eldorado* and *Oriente* series. *"Each piece from Aureliano Toso,"* it was declared on the pages of Produzione d'Arte in the 1952 issue dedicated to the Mostra del vetro Muranese, *"portrays in a rhapsodic tale the most unbelievable colors from the world of nature. A fresh look is among the principles for the inspiration which moves Dino Martens*

to rediscover the color of Murano glass" (Produzione d'arte 1952, 13-14).

The extroverted artist Fulvio Bianconi collaborated assiduously with Venini in the early post-war years creating numerous collections with a decidedly painterly concept. He created the famous vessels, the vividly colored *pezzati, a fasce verticali, a macchie, scozzesi,* and the noted series of figurines with some of the characters taken from the *commedia dell'arte*. With Bianconi, Paolo Venini himself took to designing new glass works for which he used sophisticated *murrine* and rods of *zanfirico*, which, as Domus recalls, *"were widely appreciated even at the foreign exhibitions Venini participated in (Stockholm, London, Helsinki) (....)"* (Domus 1955, April). Venini & C. met considerable success at the 1954 Triennale in Milan. The young architect Massimo Vignelli, who had been working for the company for several years, designed the 4000 series lamps of which the *Fungo* was awarded the Compasso d'Oro. In addition to the many designers who actively worked on Murano in the 50s, one must not forget the role played by two gifted glassmakers—owners of their own furnaces—who constantly dedicated their time to experimentation and to the development of glass techniques which explored the material's potential.

If Alfredo Barbini, ideal student of Napoleone Martinuzzi, showed a marked preference for *massiccio* glass, Archimede Seguso was a major innovator of the *filigrana* technique. His *merletto* vessels became the characteristic sign of his work during the 60s.

Ercole Barovier, a tireless creator of new collections for his furnace, also presented new pieces during the late 50s and 60s which stood for their variety of compositions in multi-colored glass *tessere*.

The richness of color that had been characteristic of glass production during the 50s progressively gave way—during the 60s and 70s—to a sober singleness of color. Hence, the choice of transparent glass: it was more compatible with the tendencies of modern design which sought a greater essentiality of form.

One of the glass workshops which best represented this new orientation was, without a doubt, Vetreria Vistosi. Vistosi established itself with monochromatic pieces which, only rarely, were decorated with *murrine*. Most of the Murano glass workshops encountered some difficulty in dealing with this minimalism which necessarily meant abandoning traditional glass techniques and the manual skill that went with them.

Of all the glass workshops, Venini & C., where Ludovico Diaz de Santillana became director after the death of his father-in-law Paolo Venini (1959), remained faithful to the polychromatic, or multi-colored tradition of Murano. The new artistic director did not alter the course set by its founder and maintained the openness it was known for by continuing to call in new collaborators. In the 60s, many new designers came to Venini & C. Tobia Scarpa gave his own personal reading of the ancient technique of *murrine* in a contemporary key. Massimo Vignelli renewed his collaboration with the company by designing pieces of refined formal strictness.

And then there was the American Thomas Stearns, who may claim fatherhood of pieces executed with the *incalmo* technique. These latter pieces, together with the *vetro e argento* series by Massimo Vignelli, appeared in an article in Domus in 1963 which once again pointed out *"...besides the beauty of the forms (....),* (there is) *the continuity of the spirit of invention and experimentation, and the continuity of excellence which repeatedly characterize Venini's work"* (Domus 1963, July).

Work produced for the Venini & C. by the Italian Toni Zuccheri and the Finnish Tapio Wirkkala also proved to be significant. The first, Zuccheri, created a brightly colored collection of birds and farmyard animals as well as vessels inspired by the vegetable world.

The second, Wirkkala, created very light but extraordinarily well-manufactured pieces. From the 70s onward, Venini & C. was able to rely on the research conducted by a new generation of artists who came to work in the furnace sporadically. Many young Americans came to Murano during this period: among them were Tina Marie Aufiero, Dale Chihuly, James Carpenter, Dan Dailey, Marvin Lipfsky, Richard Marquis, Benjamin Moore, John Milner, Michael Nourot, William Prindle and Toots Zynsky. All contributed to the vitality of Venini, as did Laura Diaz de Santillana who began working with the Venini glass workshop in the mid 70s.

Murano is, today, in sync with the American Studio Glass. Over the past decades, traditional production from Murano is giving way to a new reality authored by new artists/designers who use glass to create true works of art. Some of them come from the world of the furnace and have chosen this unique material for their own artistic expression—such as Lino Tagliapietra, Laura Diaz de Santillana and Yoichi Ohira. Others, like Cristiano Bianchin, have come to glass in the search for new experiences.

Made personally by the artists, or in collaboration with skilled *maestri*, Venetian glass has—and still is—being used to create works which are shown in international art exhibitions and many pieces maintain their rightful place in some of the most important art collections. And, as evidenced by the Nancy Olnick & Giorgio Spanu Collection, they are the basis for a collection in its entirety. Thus, the art of Venetian glass is spread throughout the world, continuing to make its enduring—and most fortunate—contribution.

Lino Tagliapietra, inheritor of the centuries old Muranese tradition, known worldwide as one of the most influential interpreters of contemporary glass.

Not one without the other
The collaboration between Artist and Craftsman
in Muranese glass

Susanne K. Frantz, *Former Curator of 20th Century Glass,*
The Corning Museum of Glass

Throughout most of the 3,500-year history of glass, objects have been designed and made by the same person. Although there are exceptions to this tradition, it was not until the second half of the 19th century that architects and artists began to exert a presence as designers. At that time it was not unusual for a design to originate from an individual who was unfamiliar with the physical properties of glass and the intricacies of its fabrication. An object could go from drawing board to showroom without any direct communication between the designer and glassmaker. The results sometimes suffered. Eventually a different way of working developed, one that fostered a closer collaboration between artist and artisan.

Emile Gallé, working in France at the turn of the 20th century, and one of the greatest artists to ever choose the material, did not blow glass. His most personal and idiosyncratic creations could only be the result of an extended face-to-face dialogue at the furnace with the glassblower. The 1910s and 1920s ushered in the now standard manufacturing procedure of artists, architects, and professional designers working closely with craftsmen on the factory floor.

Imagine the interior of a factory where handmade glass is made. Usually it is a surprisingly small space swarming with people who dodge between one another and around the equipment. The temperature is uncomfortably warm and the furnaces are roaring. Each person is a member of a team that serves one bench where a senior glassblower (*maestro*) presides. The jobs are defined by a centuries-old protocol: preparation of the "gather" of molten glass from the furnace; assisting the glassblower; transferring the glass from the blower's pipe to the pontil rod; and transporting the finished glass to the annealing oven for cooling.

Amid this complicated orchestra, the designer steps in to develop the prototype that will serve as a guide for subsequent production. He or she usually brings a drawing, model, or template that can range in refinement from a rough sketch to a detailed schematic. Some arrive with nothing but an idea that is described orally. There is first a discussion in which the glassmaker offers suggestions on how the object might be made more gracefully and efficiently. The experiments begin with possible modifications sketched out in chalk on the furnace or scratched on the floor. The designer directs and asks for changes. Sometimes a mistake—a slight bulge or a misaligned handle—inspires a revision to the original concept. Should the foot be wider? Can the stem and bowl be connected with a flat patty of glass, or would a hollow sphere be stronger and more elegant? Every step of the way must be discussed and approved. Sometimes there is frustration generated by the repeated attempts of one person to realize the vision of another. Eventually a design is either abandoned or a solution is reached that permits the object to go into production within an acceptable price range. For objects that are unique or issued in limited editions, the cost is less of an issue.

In 19th and early 20th century Italy, glass craftsmen took their design inspiration from the past. They revived and embellished historical forms and they largely ignored contemporary trends. As was true in Scandinavia and other parts of Europe, the 1920s through the 1960s brought forth stunning new developments—most often the result of teaming an artist or architect with excellent glassmakers.

Those decades are identified with a handful of designers who had an incomparable influence on the modernization of Italian glass.

In the 1910s and 1920s it was painter Vittorio Zecchin working with Artisti Barovier and then Cappellin Venini & C. Vetri Soffiati Muranesi. The late 1920s and the 1930s were dominated by sculptor Napoleone Martinuzzi, then architect Carlo Scarpa guided the artistic direction of Venini during the later 1930s until 1947. Fulvio Bianconi took over from Scarpa and defined the look of the company in the 1950s. Such designers as Massimo Vignelli and Tapio Wirkkala introduced the more minimal, lighter styling and the subtle color palette that characterized the 1960s.

Countless others, both Italian and foreign, relied on the superbly skilled craftsmen to help form a canon of objects. Carlo Scarpa, in particular, is remembered by many as displaying great respect for the glassmakers and for seeking out their opinions. During the 1930s, glassblower Alfredo Barbini worked closely with Napoleone Martinuzzi. Both Barbini and Archimede Seguso executed the designs of Flavio Poli. For almost forty years Fulvio Bianconi worked with one of Venini's most remarkable *maestri*, Arturo Biasutto, known as "Boboli." Boboli's ability to execute difficult shapes remains legendary in Murano. So, too, the skills of another great craftsman, Carlo Tosi, called "Caramea," who specialized in blowing the most intricate and exquisite goblets. Just a few of the other glassmakers who played important roles include Giuseppe and Benvenuto Barovier, Aldo "Polo" Bon, Aldo Nason, Ermanno Nason, Mario "Grasso" Tosi, Ermete Toso, and Licio Zuffi. While the names of numerous designers are familiar today, unfortunately most of the craftsmen remain relatively unknown outside of Murano. Some people subscribe to the theory that glass can only be effectively designed by a person who is thoroughly familiar with the craft of glassmaking. Only through experience with the physical capabilities of the medium can its natural qualities be fully exploited. Others hold to the idea that it is sometimes better for the designer to be less familiar with technique. He or she comes to a project with fresh eyes and is not restricted by the past. That designer may not accept the words, "It is not possible." By insisting on bending the rules of tradition, new ground is sometimes broken.

Thomas Stearns, an American in Venice on a Fulbright travel scholarship and a grant from the Italian government, was one such artist. He did not arrive as an aspiring glassblower or even as an aspiring designer—rather, Stearns came to Venini as an artist fascinated by the material. He wished to investigate glass as a medium for art—specifically one that he could use to record his impressions of Venice. From late 1960 through most of 1962, he stood with the glassmakers every day—explaining, arguing, and learning. When he urged them to make asymmetrical vessels and place the openings off-axis, he was asking them to go against everything they were taught. Stearns pushed them to work with difficult glasses and to use a subdued color palette that was "not Venetian." The results were unprecedented in their intimacy. Stearns attributes much of his success to his good fortune at working with the young maestro Francesco "Checco" Ongaro. Ongaro was unusual in several ways: he was willing to experiment with complex designs and enjoyed the challenge of inventing new ways to fabricate shapes. He also possessed a natural curiosity and welcomed the peculiar input of a foreign artist. Stearns recalls, *"Checco's skills were just short of incredible. He could smoothly and quickly shift between making thinly blown small pieces to those that were heavy and large."* Ultimately, Ongaro had a significant impact on the development of American studio glass through his work with students eager to learn Muranese glassmaking techniques. Dan Dailey, Richard Marquis, Benjamin Moore, Michael Nourot, and Toots Zynsky are among those who benefited from Ongaro's graciousness and expertise.

Beginning in the 1950s, entrepreneur Egidio Costantini solicited designs from well-known painters and sculptors throughout the world. He called his enterprise "La Fucina degli Angeli" and introduced a somewhat different relationship between designer and craftsman. Most of the artists who responded to his requests had no experience with glass and little or no involvement in the actual manufacture of the pieces. Instead, the designs were interpreted by Costantini and, perhaps more significantly, by the glassmakers he employed, such as *maestro* Loredano Rosin. Some designers take the glass into their own hands. During the late 1940s, Fulvio Bianconi produced prototype vessels by cutting the glass himself. The deeply gouged forms are almost primitive in their look and suggest stone or wood sculptures. Such items can only be produced by the direct intervention of the artist. From the mid-1940s, German-born Erwin Walter Burger, based in Milan, ran his own studio where he carved figures and animals from solid blocks of glass cullet. Nevertheless, the long-standing tradition of the artist/craftsman has strongly survived in glassmaking. Individuals such as Archimede Seguso and Alfredo Barbini are admired for producing their own designs as well as fabricating the designs of others. Seguso started his own company in 1946 and Barbini established his in 1950. Both acted as chief designer and glassblower over the following decades. Lino Tagliapietra is also an example of extreme flexibility and talent. Tagliapietra worked for years as a blower in the Muranese glass industry and was noted for his exceptional skill. In 1986 he began working freelance with artists to execute their designs. With others, such as Dan Dailey, he works even more closely to produce a synthesis of the aesthetics of both participants. Today, Tagliapietra concentrates on his own designs which, while deeply rooted in the colorful Italian styles of the 1940s and 1950s, are interpretations that have redefined the look of modern Italian glass. The craftsman's critical role is becoming more widely acknowledged. A few artists, such as Yoichi Ohira, are publicly acknowledging their work as the result of an equal partnership. Ohira is atypical in that his pieces are signed with his own name and that of the glassmaker with whom he has collaborated since 1993, Livio "Maisasio" Serena.

All of the ancient traditions still flourish in Murano today.

The artist/craftsman continues to make his (and occasionally her, for things change slowly on the island) designs. Professional designers employed by the glass companies still stand next to the glassblower and work out product prototypes. Local and foreign artists who have chosen glass as their medium also make the boat journey to Murano. They are privileged to hire some of the world's finest glassmakers to help develop and realize ideas that would otherwise be impossible to produce. Whatever the arrangement, there is no escaping the absolute interdependence of designer and craftsperson. In the finest work, the craftsman is much more than a simple tool for replicating a drawing. Each and every design should represent a conversation and a negotiation between artist, maker, and the glass.

Alfredo Barbini
Venice June 9, 2000

For me, giving form to the mass that glows from the heat is a joy. I do it naturally. What I like the most about the work in the furnace is the fire—the element that changes the material.

As far as I am concerned, I always analyze the harmony of the shapes, their softness, their smoothness and their delicacy.

I always have this desire to caress the glass—to shape it with my hands—the one thing that is obviously impossible. This is why I have invented *il guanto di carta bagnata* (the wet paper glove technique) which allows me to put my hands as close as possible to the molten glass. Other glassmakers use this technique and they call it *palla di carta* (paper ball).

Of the many apprentices I have had, many have not attained recognition. And that is because they preferred the economical rewards rather than the laborious, exhausting exploration into creativity that can give fruit only with time.

The most important school one can have is the workshop where the glass is worked manually. At seventeen and a half, I was already *primo maestro*. My advice to the young is to always think how rebellious, stubborn and untamed the glass is. To work it you need to make it your accomplice—you have to bend to it and understand it by anticipating what it wants to do. In this way, you give birth to the piece without forcing it.

Cristiano Bianchin
Venice March 30, 2000

Dear Nancy and Giorgio,

You have asked me to share my thoughts on glass, and I am happy to accept because it gives me the opportunity to analyze my however brief experience with this extraordinary medium. I have decided to do it with this open letter, opening myself as you have opened to the world your collection of 20th century Venetian art glass that you have put together with great passion and of which I am now part.

Personally, I think that I approached glass almost accidentally, but the results make me sure that there must be a link between the randomness of an unplanned action and the multifaceted curiosity that it can kindle. Glass is then curiosity, a game that has turned into painstaking analysis.

I don't think artists can express themselves through any medium unless they live in close daily contact with the place where the medium is brought to life. Even after many years, I feel a thrill every time I see those incredible furnaces. Here the crucibles with their red-hot hearts of molten glass are handled by men who live their life as in one of those circles in Dante's *Inferno*, where the damned move among fire, iron, sweat and curses, born to create glass out of humble minerals and become one with it. Glass is then a good vantage point as well as the most intriguing medium.

I am fascinated by the timelessness offered by the furnaces, a dimension that opens into a contemporariness that is disclosed only to the most attentive observer, and that sometimes sheds a less than magical aspect on glassmaking.

I have always been very involved in experimentation, ever since I began working both with glass and in contemporary art, and the medium is of paramount importance to convey to the viewer the sensuality implicit in my art. My hemp installations, my drawings, and my glass pieces are essential and symptomatic components of the artistic research I have been developing over the years through the different media of visual communication. Right from the start, I have worked with glass as a possible form of evolutionary continuity based on the classic validity of the Murano glassmaking techniques that I contrast with forms whose plasticity is meant to be perceived through the eyes, through touch, and lately also through hearing. This latest development in my research is meant to create a sort of perceptual filter, guiding the viewer through composite sound back to the form, which is thus reanimated.

From 1992 to 1995, the perception I had of glass urged me to actively employ the most traditional techniques. Blown glass with hot-modelled solid glass additions, *murrine* (a great passion of mine), *incalmo*, wheel engraving, stippling, wheel cutting and grinding, hot enamel applications, all were experienced as something to be tried. I felt, and to a certain extent I still feel, like someone who opens an alchemist's recipe book full of the secret formulas carefully recorded by some long gone glassmaker.

And yet, I was not entirely happy with the result. My dissatisfaction was not directed at the forms I was creating but what I was striving to achieve was an aesthetic and conceptual improvement in the forms themselves.

In late 1995 I changed the direction of the evolution of my forms, steering it toward a more precise aesthetic research, in spite of the problems this involved. The forms named *Nidi* (Nests) were conceived as mineral architectures whose surface, imagined as the careful and detailed "inscription", or a renewed "architectural description", serves an emotional, tactile condition dictated by the necessity to lay a sort of skin over the glass body, on which to leave clear yet sensual marks, animating it with an opposite and rough material like hemp. To these sculptures without a base, I added other pieces that I called *Semi* (Seeds), *Fusi* (Pods) and *Nidifusi* (Nestpods), sometimes placing them on beds of peat or clay, the natural elements on which these forms germinate. The installations represent an indefinite place and time, and sometimes even give a sense of displacement, as if this nature inhabited by artificial bodies was coming awake after an ancient sleep, re-emerging from a state that is life and death at the same time.

Between 1998 and 2000, new ideas penetrated my research, originating the *Riposapesi* (Resting Weights) and *Canestri* (Baskets). These forms are the result of the evolution of the *Nidi*, and I consider them as an essential analysis of the possible transformation of glass into "something else". The story they tell is a disquieting one, and the blown glass, either black or in saturated colours, is synthetically austere, in spite of the superimposed pieces that seem to be engaged in a sort of game. In some of these works I began to deny to the human eye the possibility of reaching the refined compactness of the glass, covering the whole surface with a thick hemp mesh that becomes once more a symbolic skin stretched over the glass bone structure.

Today I am trying to find as much time as possible to dedicate to my work in my studio in Venice. I look forward to seeing you again, and I thank you for the opportunity you have given me to express my opinion.

Best of luck for the exhibition.

Laura Diaz de Santillana
Venice May 30, 2000

I've always been entranced by the mystery of objects that reveal themselves by accident. I like things that seem impenetrable at first, only revealing themselves when you try to look at them in a different way. Glass is like a colored veil with a structure inside of it, a structure that holds it together. I am always trying to get to the center of a piece by peeling off what is not essential. Even though I use a wide range of techniques, my focus is always on purity and economy. These last pieces have a sculptural quality, but they are also two-dimensional, like paintings. Yet, to me they have more substance than paintings. The shape is the simplest of shapes; it is strong and extremely concentrated.

Benjamin Moore
Seattle May 26, 2000

The fundamental concern and focus of my blown glass is achieving simplicity, balance and clarity of form. I use color to attract attention to contour, but utilize very little surface decoration, which I feel would take away from the purity of the object's form. Opacity, translucency and transparency are elements that I vary to create different impressions for each series of works. For me the true challenge of creating an object is giving the piece a timeless presence. To this effect, I utilize several ancient Roman techniques of manipulating glass, combined with only one or two colors that vary in saturation according to the form.

The interior fold series incorporates an ancient technique of folding glass over onto itself to create a decorative element, a process that has continued to interest me since the beginning of my career. In this series, I combine this folding technique with a radiating plane of glass which is spun out from the throat of the vessel. Translucent color is used boldly to accent the contours of these vessels while letting color filter through when lit from above. A spiral wrap draws attention to the circular form.

Utilizing a similar technique, the exterior fold series is meant to be a study of form, and I prefer these vessels to be displayed as sets of three vessels. Colors for this series vary from subtle to bold and are most often transparent.

The *palla* series is my most recent body of work. I developed this series based on a simple spherical form—*palla* is the Italian word for ball. In this series, the *palla* functions as the foot of the form as well as its focal point. Contrasting colors that are usually opaque are used for this series to draw attention to the design elements. These vessels I create as pairs, including a bowl and vase shape.

In addition to my work in glass objects, I also create specialized blown glass lighting fixtures such as pendant lamps, wall sconces and floor lamps. When metal is incorporated into the design, it is created by the well-known metal artist, Louis Mueller. Through these collaborative works, we strive for a sense of balance between the formal qualities of the materials and the playfulness of many of our design concepts.

Yoichi Ohira
Meditation on glass

Venice March 15, 2000

I have loved glass since I was a little boy. In its transparency, it seemed like I could see—and not see. It gave me a glimpse of the mysterious purity of nature: the sky, the stars, the crisp clean air, the pure water, the white snow.

When I was 20 years old, while reading a book by the Japanese writer Hiroyuki Itsuki, a novel about the love between a Japanese glassmaker and a Finnish glass dealer, I discovered an extraordinary poetic connection between the transparency of glass and music without a sound. It was the kind of music that one hears with the eyes and with the heart—not with the ears. Since that moment, glass became for me synonymous with sublimated love. At 22, I was hired as an apprentice by the Kagami Crystal Company, a very well-known artistic glass workshop in Tokyo. I worked as a glassmaker so I could understand this medium directly.

While at Kagami, I saw a television program on the making of glass in Murano. I was fascinated by this island so foreign and mysterious. A few days later, I went to the library of the Istituto Italiano di Cultura in Tokyo and found a book on the island of Murano.

As I studied the many beautiful color illustrations, I was captured by the beauty of Muranese glass: "Here is where I must go," I said to myself. I have been living in Venice for the past 27 years, where I spend most of my time creating my glassworks with passion, and of course, in collaboration with two excellent *maestri*, the *soffiatore* Livio "Maisasio" Serena and the *molatore* Giacomo Barbini. What is the ideal piece of glass for me? It is a gorgeous vase that can contain a sip of the magic water of life and, perchance, will allow me to hear music without a sound.

Tobia Scarpa
A very brief note on glassmaking in Venice

Trevignano June 2, 2000

Dear Nancy and Giorgio,
You have asked me to write a note on glassmaking in Venice. It is wasted time! Look at me. Venice has finally landed in Las Vegas. The real Las Vegas. And what is left of the real Venice is really very small.

A city, to be real, must have its citizens. The citizens of Venice are almost all tourists—people passing through. And the ones that remain don't know how to make glass anymore.

Giorgio, you and Nancy are brave and you are right to love and to own the most beautiful glassworks of a particular moment—those in which a ferociously preserved tradition has been embedded in the marvel of a new thought, the modern. But the modern is seen through that particular lens that is the sensibility of the lagoon.

This sensibility has the magic of making anything beautiful and this is not a small thing. In fact, those glassworks that you love, protect and preserve have the reflection of the Venetian canals, the light of the Venetian passageways and the sound of the Venetian squares. That is all they have. The rest of Venice, you can find much more comfortably in Las Vegas.

P.S. Today June 2nd, 2000 would have been the 84th birthday of my father, Carlo Scarpa.

Thomas Stearns
by Susan Sacks

New York April 15, 2000

Thomas Stearns is a poet. He's also a teacher. A sculptor. A physicist. An engineer. A chemist. A philosopher. And humanist. His chosen form of expression happens to be light. And he captures it, teases it, and forces it to talk to us in a language we all understand. He makes it speak to us, thankfully, in glass. His fascination with light led him to be the first American to enter the sacred space of all glassblowers, Murano, who was to have designs incorporated into the Venini line. He was chosen by Paolo Venini himself, months before his death, on the basis of flatwork designs Stearns had created for windows while attending the Cranbrook Academy of Art (1957-1959). Stearns was enraptured by windows—the way light would stream through them; how its intensity could change. The designs, inspired by pictures in magazines Stearns had seen when he was in college, would earn him coveted passage across the vast psychological ocean separating his hometown of Oklahoma City from Murano. He arrived in October 1959. Unfortunately, he was never to meet the founder of Venini & C., the man who changed the course of his life, and the history of modern glass.

Upon arriving, Stearns proceeded to extend the accepted boundaries of glassblowing with conceptual techniques never before conceived much less attempted. Perhaps it was because his isolation and loneliness forced him to keep close company with his art. Image and color were his most intimate relationships. Venice exposed them to him by night and then he would tell of his experiences by day; translating them into shapes that are, at once, evocative, strong and emotional.

Knowing that Stearns does not speak one word of Italian, his brief two-year stint in the small factory outside Venice becomes even more extraordinary. His work, forged in tandem with renown glassblower *maestro* Francesco "Checco" Ongaro, takes on an even deeper meaning; the meaning of metaphor, insinuation, and trust that words, in any language, merely confuse and trivialize. Together, their patient, sweaty journey into light and form resulted in statements about life that were to change the shape of hand-blown glass for eternity. Where did he get the audacity? He will tell you it came straight from home—from being required, even at a very young age, to participate in preparations for the evening meal. Mistakes didn't matter. They ended up on the table just like everything else. And this eating of the results, no matter what shape they ended up in, encouraged a sense of confidence and creativity that stayed with him. Trial and error become not only natural. But necessary. His journey was indeed a rewarding one: his outstanding pieces winning him the coveted 31st Venice Biennale in 1962, an award never before received by an American. And although this was taken from him when it was realized that he was not from Italy, we still have the pieces that earned him this mighty distinction. And they earn it repeatedly, every time someone gets lost in the light only to find their way to a deeper, more meaningful place.

Nebbia Lunare (Mist of the Moon)
Sitting firmly and staunchly, this piece becomes a snapshot that localizes your presence in a certain location. Breaking all tradition in glass, it magically represents the traditional way to find your place via the moon, the sun and the stars.

Cappello del Doge (The Doge's Hat)
This emblematic symbol of the protector of Venice represents
the governing force of an individual. Stearns' playful interpretation
brings an unexpected humor to this quintessential icon.

La Sentinella di Venezia (The Sentinel of Venice)
This piece is reminiscent of the eternal flame. Shaped much like
a lighthouse, it is a warning. Stearns saw Venice melting because
of acid rain coming from the mainland. Air and water pollution
was evident everywhere and Stearns was concerned. Inspired by
the abstract expressionist Willem de Kooning, the piece sits firmly,
jutting out of a flat precipice like a mountain of fire and water.
Only three pieces were made as Stearns saw this work as a
sculpture and never intended it for multiple production. One was
destroyed. Only two remain. The Sentinel takes a stance.
It has an opinion.

Il vaso per le lacrime del Doge (Vessel for The Doge's Tears)
Making its debut here, this piece is a prototype that has never been
produced or exhibited before. It is a receptacle to hold the Doge's
tears. Executed in greens symbolizing, the stratification of the sludge
and slime in the silt of Venice, the cross at the top reminds one of
the pursing of lips. An insignia of the Catholic faith, it says the
receptacle is full—full to the brim with the tears of any government
official who must cry at night for what he cannot fix during the day.
The piece was designed for consideration by Cristofle.
The silver and gold aperture, designed by Thomas Stearns,
was crafted by Vincenzo Rossi.

Lino Tagliapietra
Venice, June 2000

There are people who think you can have more than one life, that
you can be reborn over and over again. Even I have this sensation
of having taken this path several times. And each time I do,
I do not deny my past lives; rather, I integrate them into my current
experience.
The last time I remember having this sensation was several years
ago and it was like a big explosion introducing me to completely
new feelings. I don't know whether to call it freedom or something
related to an even bigger consciousness.
I often find myself in foreign lands, just like Corto Maltese, the
traveller from Hugo Pratt—a figure I have always admired. He has
been, among other things, the inspiration of the names and forms
of my works. Like, for example, the sinuous canoes that look like
birds and the birds that resemble boats—objects that I define as
"flying shapes".
Just like Corto Maltese, whatever situation I am in, I try to remain
myself—a little bit Byzantine and a little bit modern—tied to
the tradition of the past but with an eye, day-after-day, toward
the future. And if I could, I would do just like Corto:
I would cut the palm of my hand so this could not be predestined.
Still alive in me is the spirit of the young apprentice:
full of enthusiasm with the desire to try a new path but always
with Him—the glass—my biggest friend. This is the one that helps
me in the most difficult moments, the one that inspires me and
will always be able to show me the path to follow.

Massimo Vignelli
New York, June 2000

In the early days of my career, my basic design culture was rooted in the predicament of the Bauhaus with a strong belief in design for mass production rather than for the few. My long exposure to the making of Murano's glass at Venini gave me the opportunity to revise and further articulate my approach to design. Working closely with glass and silver made me understand better the nature of craftsmanship, shifting my feelings somehow closer to the Wiener Werkstatte than the Bauhaus. My passion for materials and their properties goes back to those times.

Toots Zynsky
Providence, June 2000

At the suggestion of Gianni Toso, I traveled to Murano in early 1983 in search of colored canes for my work. I was just beginning to work exclusively with threads of glass. The Moretti company (now Effetre) had been known for centuries as arguably the largest supplier of mosaic glass in the world and, hence, offered an irresistibly large range of colors.

I met Alessandro Diaz de Santillana and the Venini family, who invited me to return in 1984 to their factory to work on unique pieces that would also be featured in future exhibitions. This plan changed, and instead I designed three groups of special edition pieces. The great appeal to me was three-fold: the possibility of working with the Italian glass master Checco Ongaro and his team; the opportunity to work in a hot glass studio that ran twelve tanks of different colors every day (a luxury by any standard); and spending three months in Venice.

During that time, we lived in an old stone house on the island of Torcello—a 30-minute boat ride from Murano. Our room had one window overlooking a tiny canal that meandered below. A shaft of sunlight from the lone window shown on the old desk just under it. I remember thinking what a perfect room it would be for a writer. I later found out it had been the first room where Ernest Hemingway lived when he was in Torcello. I also discovered that the old stone house had been the original Cipriani hotel.

I feel very fortunate to have spent this time at Venini and on Murano. I have returned again and again to Venice for the past seventeen years. It never loses its magic.

Catalogue of works

This catalogue is organized in chronological order, when possible, and then by designer. The date of each glasswork is based either on its first presentation at a major exhibition or, in some cases, on the year of its first publication. The name of each piece is derived from the name that appears in the catalogue of each respective workshop or by the name that appeared in period publications. According to the traditional glassmaking process of Murano, every piece is a *soffiato* (free blown glass) except where noted. Identifying marks, signatures and/or labels have been noted. All sizes are approximate. In general we have maintained the original nomenclature of Murano glass. These have been purposely put into italics and are described in the Glossary on pages 246 and 247.

Benvenuto Barovier

1. Floreale a murrine
Artisti Barovier, 1913-1914

2. Floreale a murrine
Artisti Barovier, 1919 ca.

Giuseppe Barovier

3. A murrine
Artisti Barovier, 1919 ca.

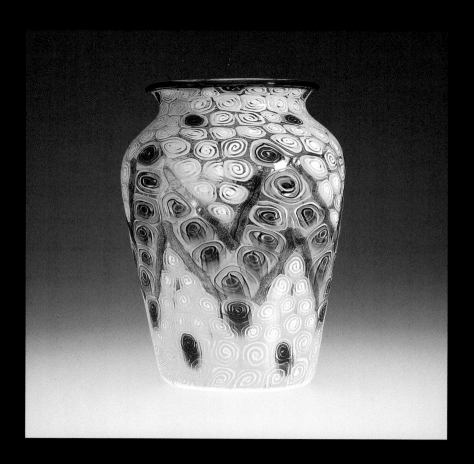

Nicoló Barovier

4. A murrine
Vetreria Artistica Barovier & C.
1924

Ercole Barovier

5. A murrine
Vetreria Artistica Barovier & C.
1927

6. Avventurina
Vetreria Artistica Barovier & C.
1929-1930

7. Primavera
Vetreria Artistica Barovier & C.
1929-1930

Vittorio Zecchin

8. Veronese
V.S.M. Cappellin Venini & C.
1921-1925

9. Trasparenti
V.S.M. Cappellin Venini & C.
1921-1925

Vittorio Zecchin

10. Trasparente
V.S.M. Cappellin Venini & C.
1921-1925

11. Libellula
V.S.M. Cappellin Venini & C.
1921-1925

Napoleone Martinuzzi

12. Trasparente
V.S.M. Venini & C., 1927 ca.

13. Pulegoso
V.S.M. Venini & C., 1930

Napoleone Martinuzzi

14. Pulegoso
V.S.M. Venini & C., 1930

15. Incamiciato
*Zecchin-Martinuzzi Vetri Artistici
& Mosaici, 1932*

16. Pasta vitrea
*Zecchin-Martinuzzi Vetri Artistici
& Mosaici, 1933*

Carlo Scarpa

17. Trasparente
M.V.M. Cappellin & C.
1926-1931

18. Trasparente
M.V.M. Cappellin & C.
1926-1931

Carlo Scarpa

19. Pasta vitrea
M.V.M. Cappellin & C.
1929-1930

20. Trasparente a ballotton
M.V.M. Cappellin & C.
1930-1931
Incamiciato
M.V.M. Cappellin & C.
1929-1930

Carlo Scarpa

21. Pasta vitrea
M.V.M. Cappellin & C.
1929-1930

22. Pasta vitrea
M.V.M. Cappellin & C.
1930

Carlo Scarpa

23. Fenicio
M.V.M. Cappellin & C.
1928-1929

24. Fenicio
M.V.M. Cappellin & C.
1930-1931

25. Pasta vitrea
M.V.M. Cappellin & C.
1929-1930
Fenicio
M.V.M. Cappellin & C.
1928-1931

Carlo Scarpa

26. Millefiori
M.V.M. Cappellin & C.
1930 - 1931
Fenici
M.V.M. Cappellin & C.
1928 - 1931

Carlo Scarpa

27. Iridato
M.V.M. Cappellin & C.
1929 - 1930

28. Lattimo
M.V.M. Cappellin & C.
1929

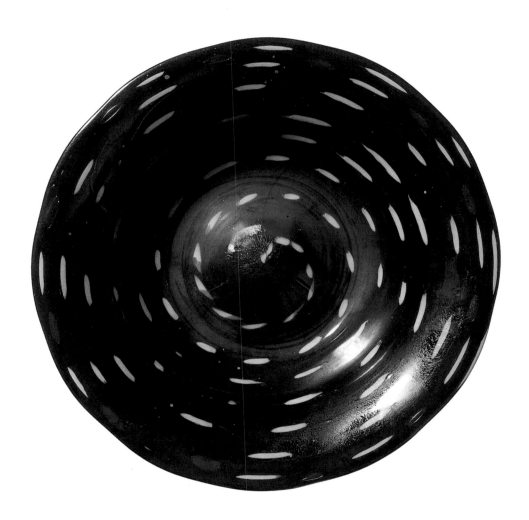

Carlo Scarpa

29. Lattimo
M.V.M. Cappellin & C., 1929

30. Lattimi
M.V.M. Cappellin & C.
1929 - 1930

Carlo Scarpa

31. Incamiciati
M.V.M. Cappellin & C., 1930

32. Incamiciato
M.V.M. Cappellin & C., 1930

Tomaso Buzzi

33. Turchese e nero
V.S.M. Venini & C., 1932

34. Alga
V.S.M. Venini & C., 1933

35. Alba
V.S.M. Venini & C., 1933

Tomaso Buzzi

36. Laguna
V.S.M. Venini & C., 1933

37. Incamiciato
V.S.M. Venini & C., 1932

Carlo Scarpa

38. A bollicine
Venini & C., 1932-1934

39. A bollicine
Venini & C., 1932-1936

Carlo Scarpa

41. Sommerso a bollicine
Venini & C., 1934-1936

42. Sommersi a bollicine
Venini & C., 1934-1936

Carlo Scarpa

44. Mezza filigrana
Venini & C., 1934-1936

45. Lattimo
Venini & C., 1934-1936

Carlo Scarpa

46. Corrosi
Venini & C., 1936

47. Corrosi
Venini & C., 1936

Carlo Scarpa

48. Murrine romane
Venini & C., 1936

49. Soffiato trasparente
Venini & C., 1936

Carlo Scarpa

50. A fasce
Venini & C., 1938

51. Variegato zigrinato
Venini & C., 1938

Carlo Scarpa

52. Tessuto
Venini & C., 1940

53. Tessuto
Venini & C., 1940

54. Tessuto
Venini & C., 1940

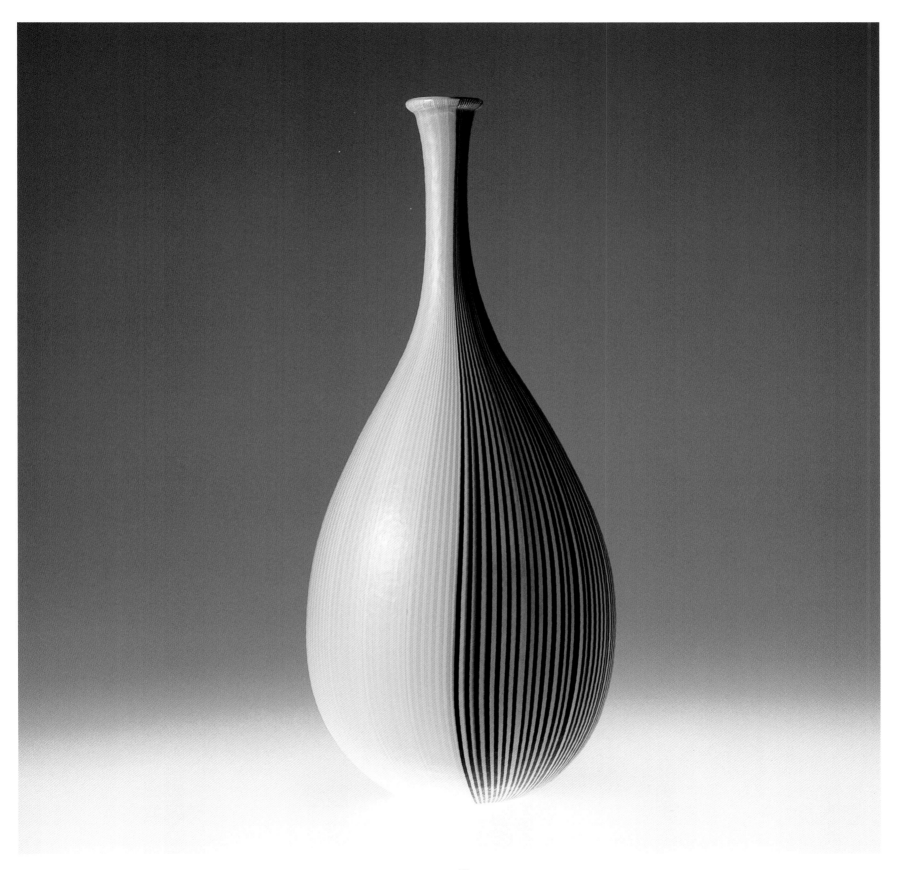

Carlo Scarpa

55. Laccati rossi e neri
Venini & C., 1940

Carlo Scarpa

56. Granulare
Venini & C., 1940

57. Iridati
Venini & C., 1940

Carlo Scarpa

58. Cinesi
Venini & C., 1940

59. Cinesi
Venini & C., 1940

Carlo Scarpa

60. Inciso
Venini & C., 1940

61. Velato e Inciso
Venini & C., 1940

62. Battuto
Venini & C., 1940

Carlo Scarpa

63. Velato
Venini & C., 1940

64. Battuti
Venini & C., 1940

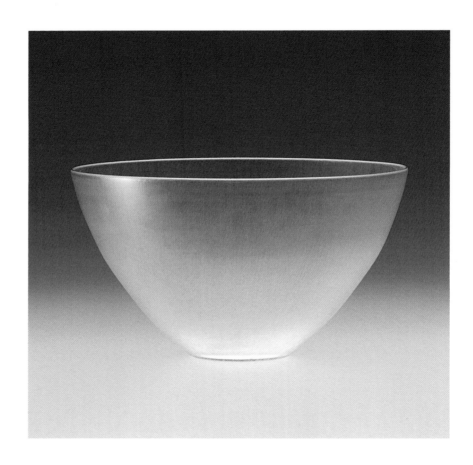

65. Murrine opache
Venini & C., 1940

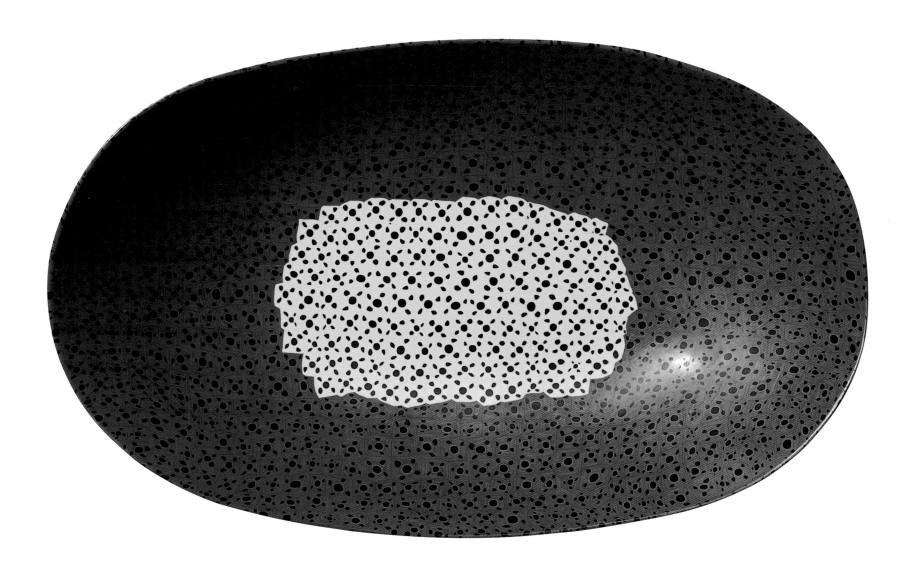

Carlo Scarpa   **66. Murrine opache**
Venini & C., 1940

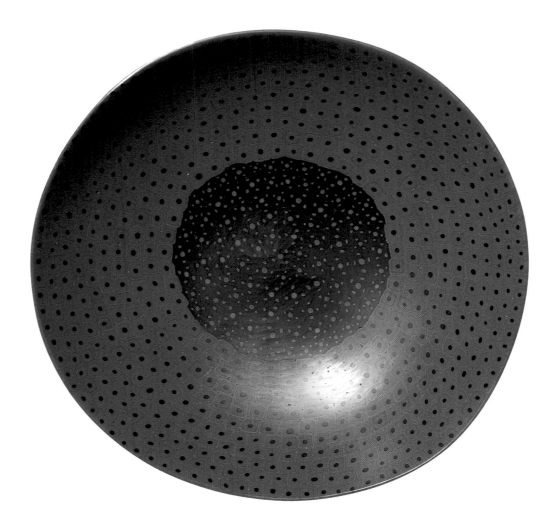

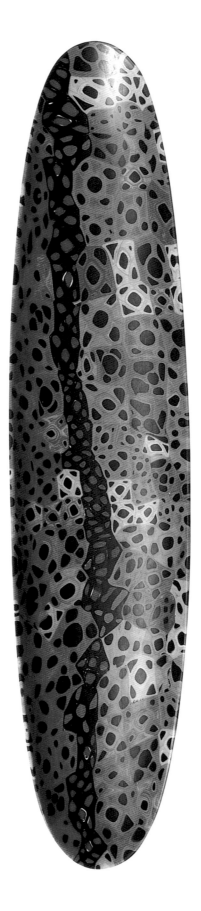

Carlo Scarpa

67. A murrine
Venini & C., 1940 ca.
Piatto del serpente
Venini & C., 1940

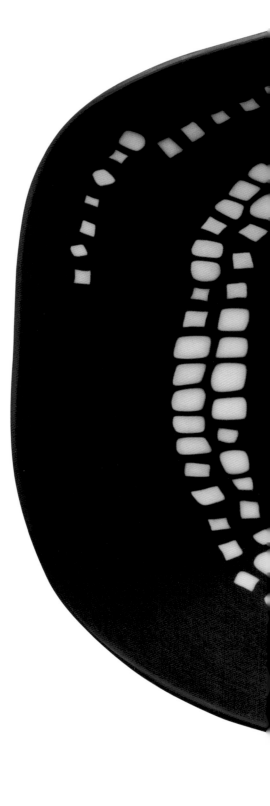

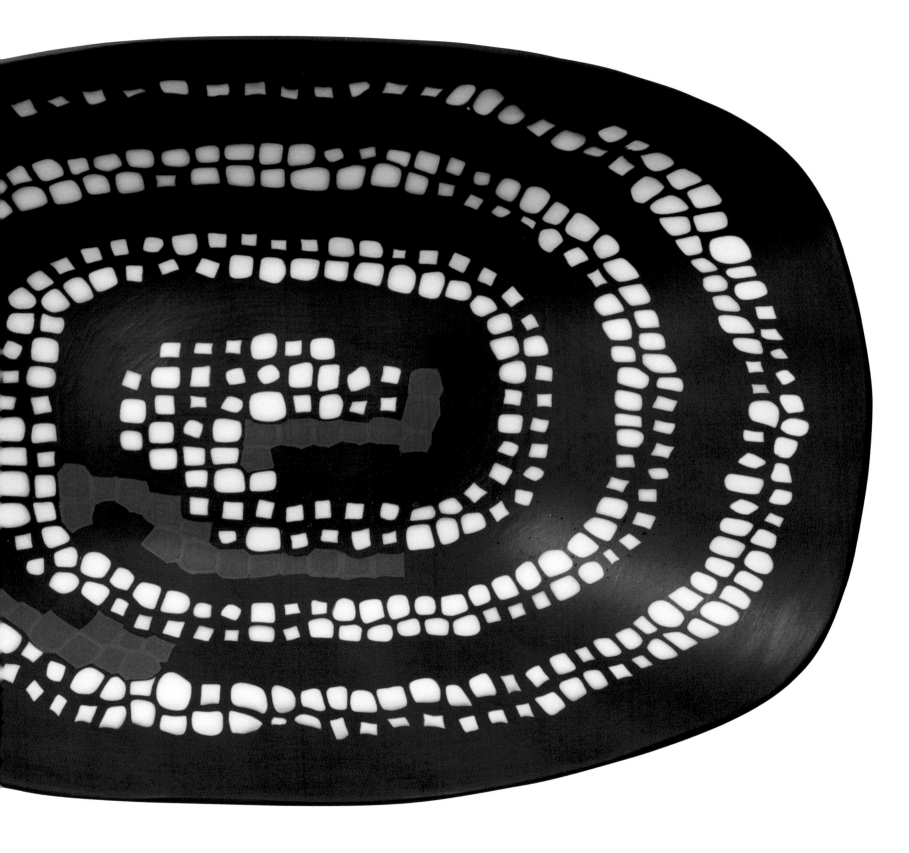

Carlo Scarpa **68. A fasce**
Venini & C., 1942

Carlo Scarpa

70. A fasce applicate
Venini & C., 1940

71. A fasce
Venini & C., 1942

Carlo Scarpa

72. A pennellate
Venini & C., 1942

73. A pennellate
Venini & C., 1942

Carlo Scarpa

74. A pennellate
Venini & C., 1942

Carlo Scarpa

75. Decoro a fili
Venini & C., 1942

Giò Ponti

77. Bottiglie morandiane
Venini & C., 1946-1950

78. Bottiglie morandiane
Venini & C., 1946-1950

79. Bottiglie morandiane
Venini & C., 1946-1950

**Fulvio Bianconi and
Paolo Venini**

80. Fazzoletti
Venini & C., 1948 ca.

81. Fazzoletti
Venini & C., 1948-1950

Fulvio Bianconi and Paolo Venini

82. Fazzoletti
Venini & C., 1950 ca.

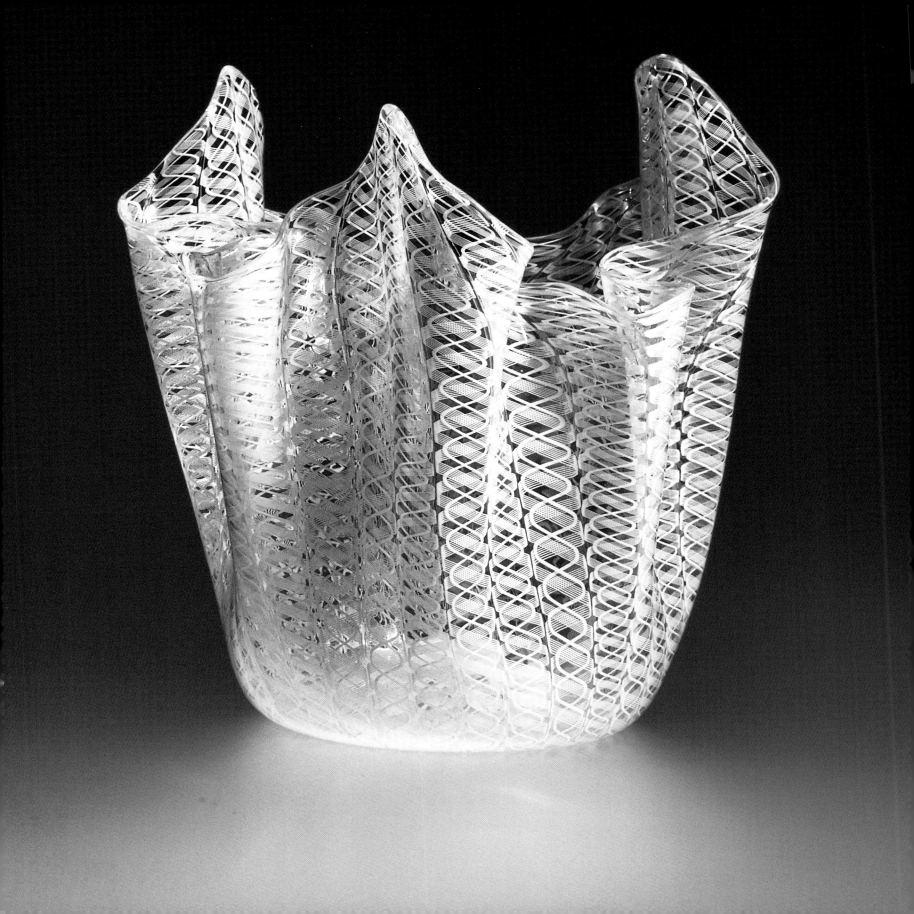

Fulvio Bianconi

83. A macchie
Venini & C., 1950

84. A spicchi
Venini & C., 1950

Fulvio Bianconi

85. Pezzato
Venini & C., 1951

86. Pezzato
Venini & C., 1950-1951

Fulvio Bianconi

88. Sirena
Venini & C., 1950

89. A fasce orizzontali
Venini & C., 1951

Fulvio Bianconi

90. A fasce orizzontali
Venini & C., 1953

91. A canne
Venini & C., 1951

Fulvio Bianconi

92. A fasce e a canne
Venini & C., 1951-1956

93. A fasce
Venini & C., 1950

94. A fasce orizzontali
Venini & C., 1951-1956

Fulvio Bianconi

95. Sasso
Venini & C., 1965

96. Informale
Venini & C., 1968

Paolo Venini

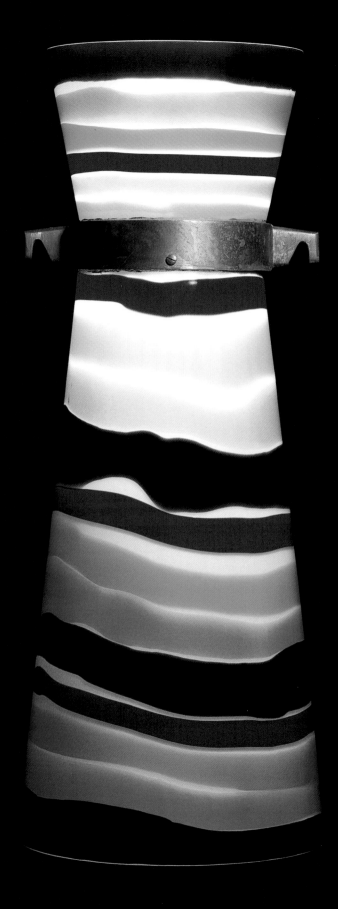

101. Sigaro
Venini & C., 1954

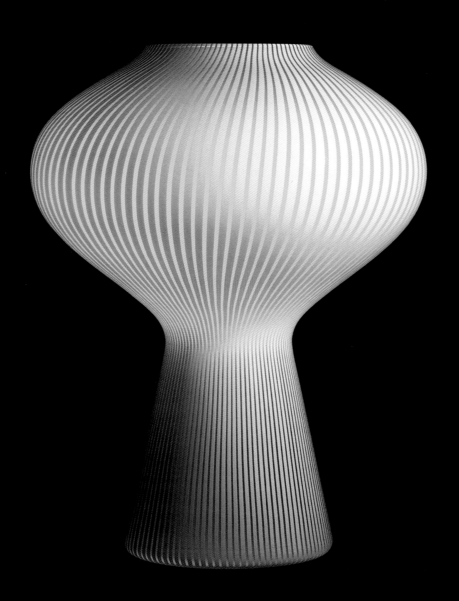

Massimo Vignelli

105. Bicchieri e Brocca Ciga
Venini & C., 1979

Dino Martens

108. Eldorado
Aureliano Toso, 1952-1954

109. Zanfirico
Aureliano Toso, 1952

Flavio Poli

112. Valva
Seguso Vetri D'Arte, 1954

113. Composizione Lattimo
Vetreria Archimede Seguso
1954

114. Merletto
Vetreria Archimede Seguso
1952

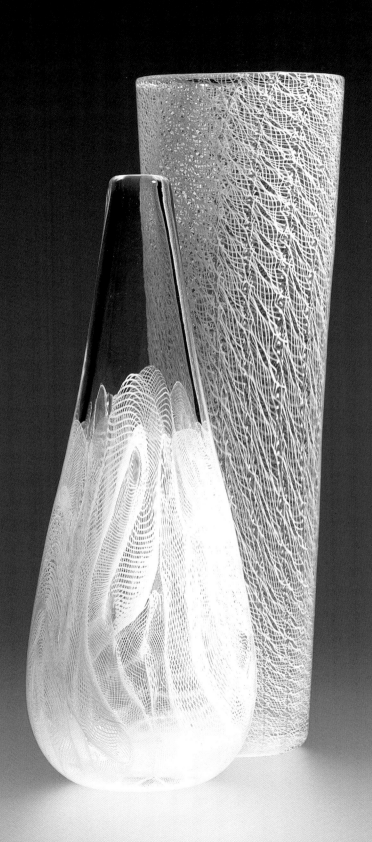

Archimede Seguso

116. Polveri
Vetreria Archimede Seguso
1953

Archimede Seguso

117. Ritorto a coste
Vetreria Archimede Seguso
1950

118. Sfumato
Vetreria Archimede Seguso
1954

Ermanno Toso

119. Murrine spiraliformi
Fratelli Toso, 1960-1962

120. Kiku
Fratelli Toso, 1959-1960

Ercole Barovier

121. Barbarico
Barovier & Toso, 1951

122. Barbarico
Barovier & Toso, 1951

Ercole Barovier

123. Eugeneo
Barovier & Toso, 1951

124. Neolitico
Barovier & Toso, 1954

125. Striati
Barovier & Toso, 1954

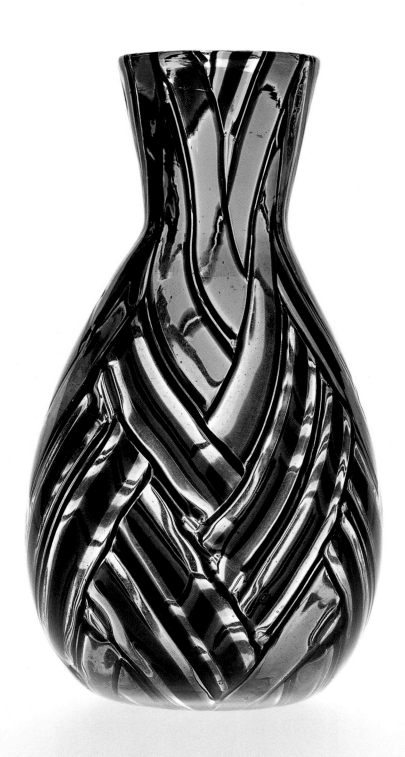

Ercole Barovier

129. Caccia
Barovier & Toso, 1962

130. Tessere Policrome
Barovier & Toso, 1962

Ercole Barovier

131. Christian Dior
Barovier & Toso, 1969

132. Rotellato
Barovier & Toso, 1970

Alfredo Barbini

133. Vetro pesante
Vetreria Alfredo Barbini, 1962

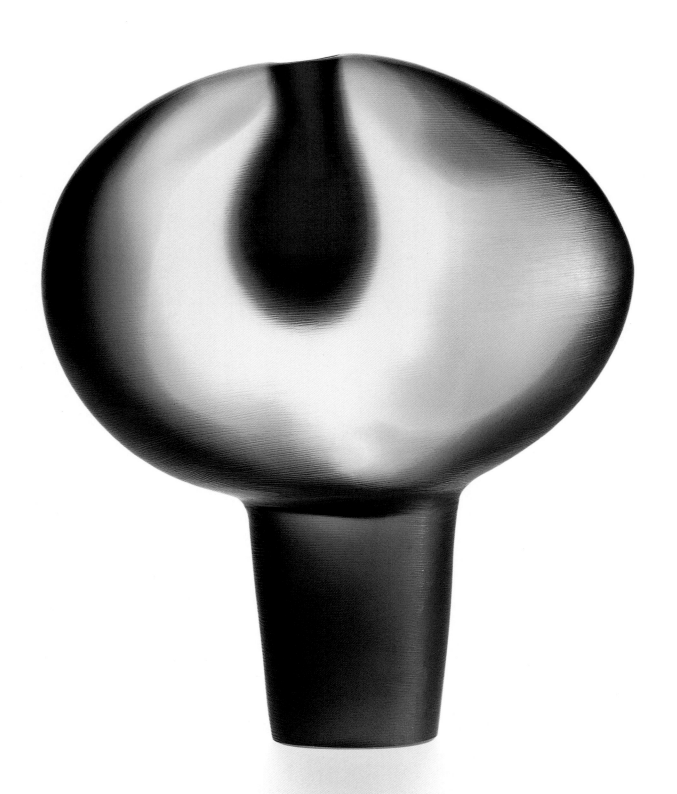

Ludovico Diaz de Santillana

134. Cannette
Venini & C., 1962

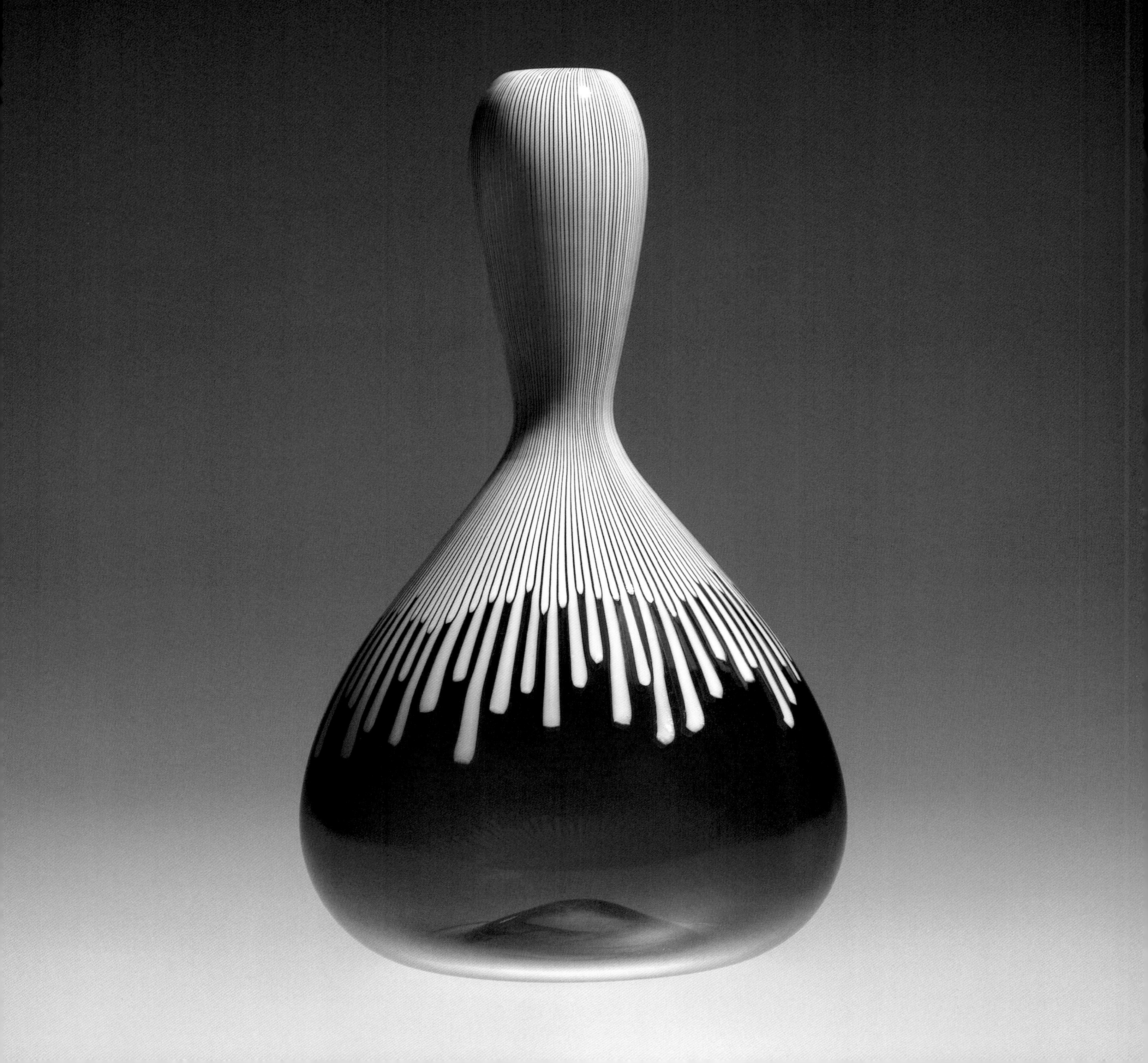

135. A murrine
1960

Venini & C.

136. A murrine
1960

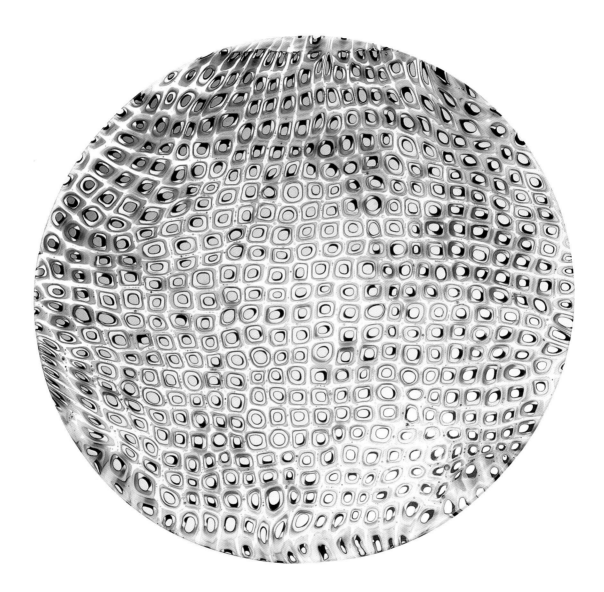

Thomas Stearns

139. Nebbia lunare
Venini & C., 1962

140. La sentinella di Venezia
Venini & C., 1962

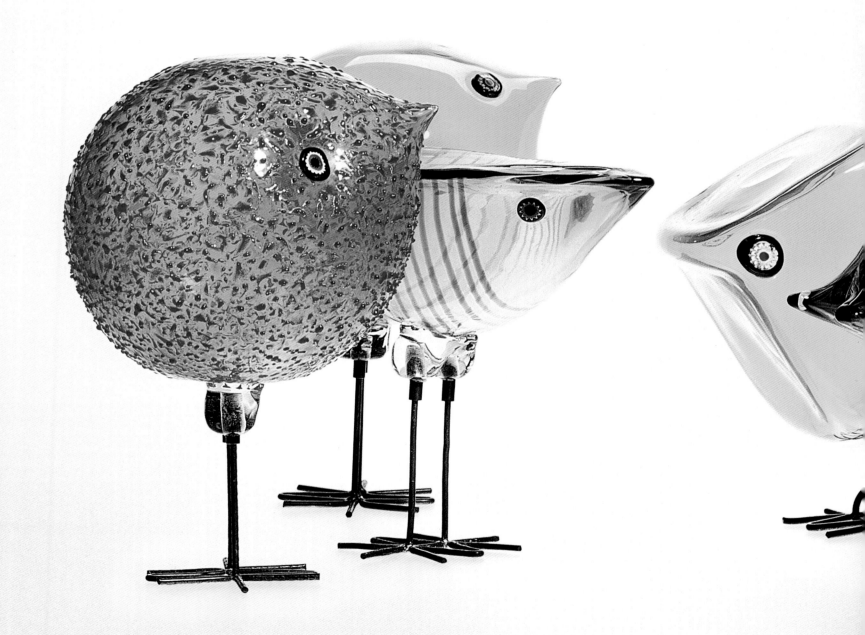

144. Fiori
Aureliano Toso, 1968 ca.

James Carpenter

147. Vetro Tessuto
Venini & C., 1979 ca.

148. Prototipo
Venini & C., 1979 ca.

James Carpenter

149. Calabash
Venini & C., 1980

150. Calabash
Venini & C., 1980

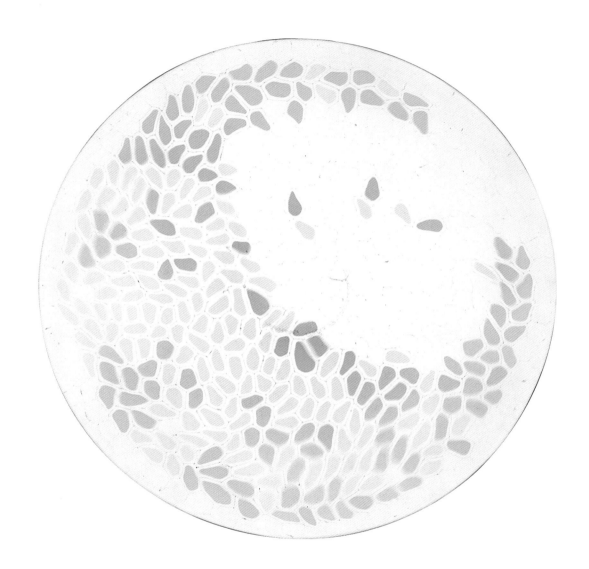

Toots Zynsky

155. Folto
Venini & C., 1984

156. Folto
Venini & C., 1984

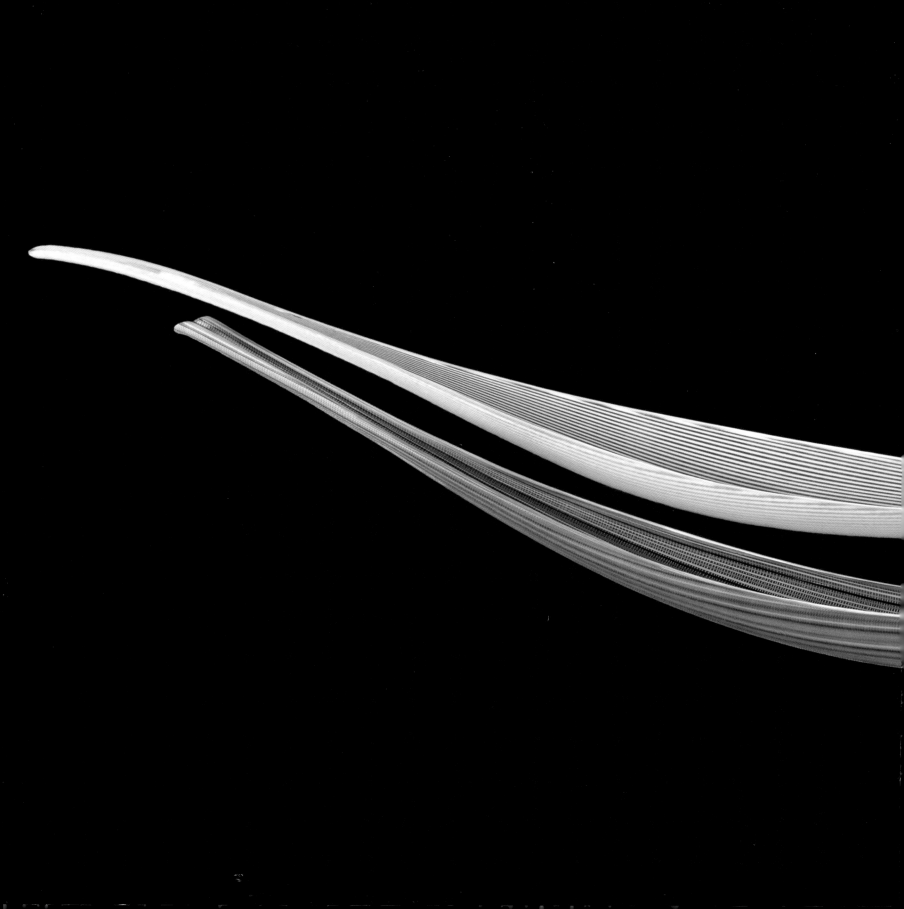

157. Boats
1998

Yoichi Ohira

158. Polveri
1997

159. Pasta vitrea
1997

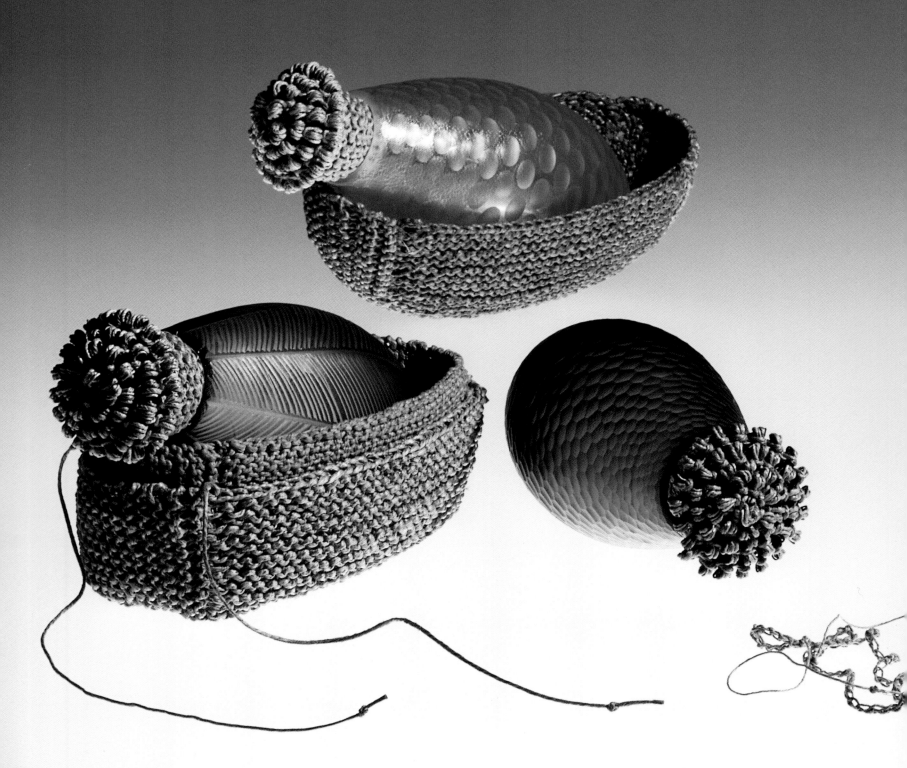

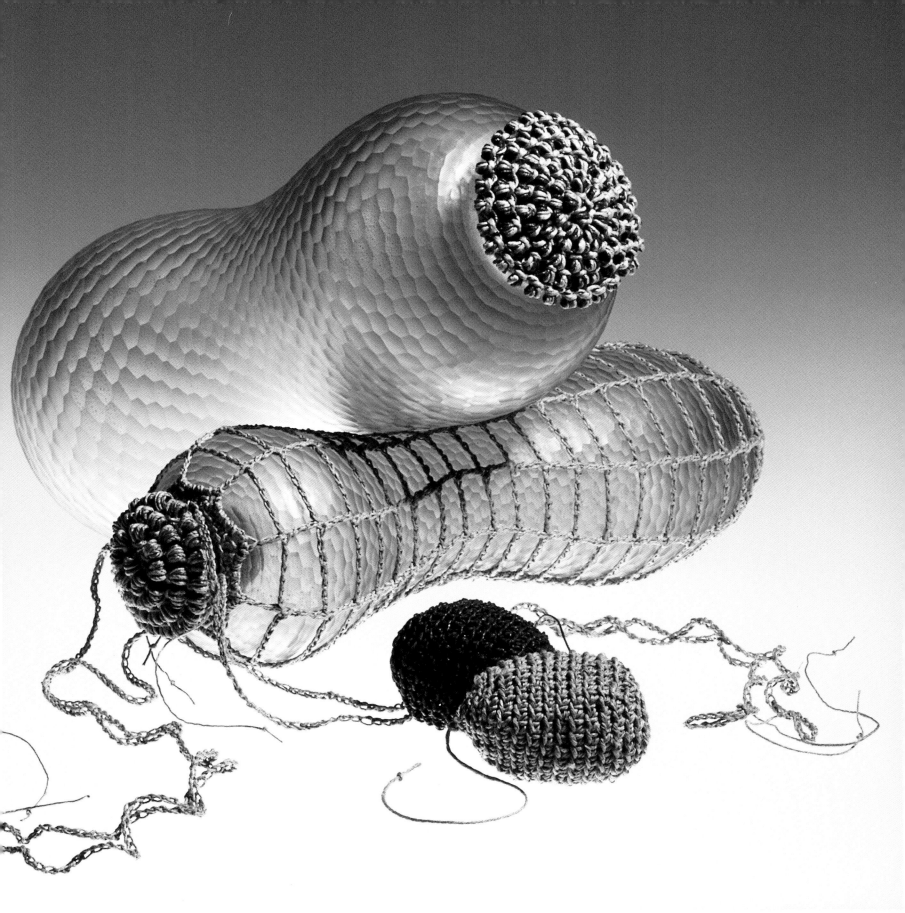

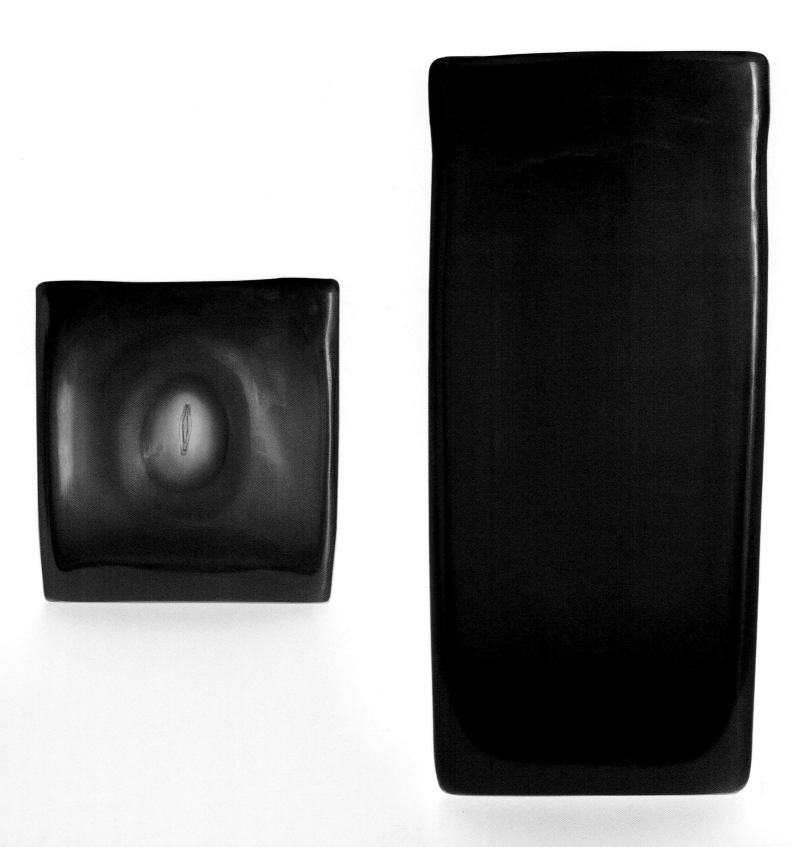

Laura Diaz de Santillana

164. T5 L' occhio
1999

165. T15
1999

166. S3, S4, S2
1999

1. Benvenuto Barovier
Artisti Barovier

Floreale a murrine, 1913-1914

Vetro mosaico vase composed of multicolored patches of translucent glass *tessere* arranged to form a floral pattern. Several vases in *vetro mosaico* were presented by the Artisti Barovier at the Ca' Pesaro show in 1913. At this exhibition the Artisti Barovier shared a room, dedicated exclusively to glass, with Vittorio Zecchin, who also designed vessels and tiles using the *murrine*

technique.
Signed with a glass *murrina* bearing the initials *AB*, above which rises a crown.
5" high (cm. 12)

Exhibitions:
1913, Venice, Ca' Pesaro (?);
1914, Venice, 11th Biennale Internazionale d'Arte (?).

Bibliography and comparative texts:
Catalogo della Esposizione di Estate, 1920, p.1;
H. Ricke, 1990, n. 371;
M. Barovier, 1993, nn. 32, 48;

M. Barovier, R. Barovier Mentasti, A. Dorigato 1995, n. 9;
M. Heiremans, 1996, n. 5.

Vase in *vetro mosaico* published in the *Catalogo della Esposizione di Estate, 1920*. Opera Bevilacqua la Masa.

2. Benvenuto Barovier
Artisti Barovier

Floreale a murrine, 1919 ca.

Vetro mosaico vase cased in *lattimo* glass, crafted with multicolored patches of translucent glass *tessere* arranged to form a floral pattern.
10" high (cm. 25)

Bibliography and comparative texts:
G. Lorenzetti, 1921, p. 1093;
M. Barovier, 1993, n. 55.

Vases in cased *vetro mosaico* published in *Le Vie d'Italia, 1921*, October.

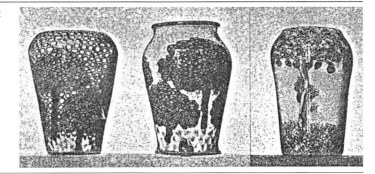

3. Giuseppe Barovier
Artisti Barovier

A murrine, 1919 ca.

A *vetro mosaico* vase crafted with spiraling white and yellow and white and red *murrine*. The central part is decorated with a stripe of *avventurina* glass, creating a *greca* pattern with the use of white and blue *murrine*.
Signed with a glass *murrina* bearing the initials *AB*, above which rises a crown.
11.25" high (cm. 27)

Bibliography and comparative texts:
R. Barovier Mentasti, 1992, n. 38;
M. Barovier, 1993, n. 50;
M. Barovier, 1994, n. 1;
M. Barovier, 1999, p. 93.

4. Nicolò Barovier
Vetreria Artistica Barovier & C.

A murrine, 1924

A *vetro mosaico* vase crafted with multicolored translucent *tessere* and canes. The *tessere* are arranged to create an extraordinary decorative pattern.
Engraved: *N. Barovier Murano*.
12.5" high (cm. 32)

Bibliography and comparative texts:
R. Barovier Mentasti, 1977, n. 2;
A. Dorigato, 1989, n. 2;
R. Barovier Mentasti, 1992, n. 40;
M. Barovier, 1993, n. 66.

Vase in *vetro mosaico*; photo from the Barovier & Toso archives, 1924.

5. Ercole Barovier
Vetreria Artistica Barovier & C.

A murrine, 1927

An amethyst vase decorated with circular red and *avventurina murrine* arranged in groups of three.
7.25" high (cm. 18.5)

Exhibitions:
1952, Venice, 26th Biennale Internazionale d'Arte, Historic exhibition of Murano glass.

Bibliography and comparative texts:
Gasparetto, 1960, n. 3;
Mostra del Vetro..., 1984, n. 126;
A. Dorigato, 1989, n. 7;
M. Barovier, 1993, n. 79;
M. Barovier, 1999, p. 103.

Barovier display at the Historic Exhibition of Murano Glass, 26th Biennale Internazionale d'Arte, Venice, 1952.

6. Ercole Barovier
Vetreria Artistica Barovier & C.

Avventurina, 1929 -1930

A vase decorated with *avventurina* glass. Applied double-curved handles *a morise* in *cristallo* glass. The vase is a variation of a model found in the *primavera* glass series.
11.25" (cm. 28)

Bibliography and comparative texts:
A. Dorigato, 1989, n. 20;
F. Deboni, 1996, p. 30.

Vase in *primavera* glass; photo from Barovier & Toso archives, 1930 ca.

7. Ercole Barovier
Vetreria Artistica Barovier & C.

Primavera, 1929 -1930

A compote in *primavera* glass with applied leaves and trim in black glass. *Primavera* glass, a milky-looking seemingly *craquelé* glass, had a very limited production. Its composition was the result of an accidental mixture of chemicals that was impossible to replicate.
8.5" high (cm. 21.5)

Exhibitions:
1930, Monza, 4th Esposizione Internazionale delle Arti Decorative e Industriali Moderne;
1930, Venice, 17th Biennale Internazionale d'Arte.

Bibliography and comparative texts:
La Casa Bella, 1930, May, pp. 50, 51;
La Casa Bella, 1930, June, pp. 56, 57;
A. Dorigato, 1989, pp. 18, 19;
M. Barovier, 1993, n. 92;
M. Heiremans, 1993, n. 34;
R. Barovier Mentasti, 1994, n. 21.

Works in *primavera* glass; photo from Barovier & Toso archives, 1930 ca.

8. Vittorio Zecchin,
V.S.M. Cappellin Venini & C.

Veronese, 1921-1925

Veronese vase in transparent amethyst glass. Vittorio Zecchin was inspired by a similar vase that appears in L'Annunciazione by the painter Paolo Veronese which is exhibited in Venice at the Museum Gallerie dell'Accademia. This vase became the logo of the Venini workshop.
13.25" high (cm. 37)

Exhibitions:
1923, Monza, 1st Esposizione Internazionale delle Arti Decorative;
1924, Venice, 14th Biennale Internazionale d'Arte (?).

Bibliography and comparative texts:
R. Linzeler, 1922, p. 666;
C. Carrà, 1923, p. 67;
R. Linzeler, 1923, p. 83;
R. Papini, 1930, n. 570;
G. Mariacher, 1967, p. 98;
R. Barovier Mentasti, 1982, n. 252;
Mille anni..., 1982, n. 503;
F. Deboni, 1984, p. n. 70;
W. Neuwirth, 1987, nn. 7, 104;

A. Dorigato, 1986, p. 71;
F. Deboni, 1989, n. 1;
L'arte del vetro, 1982, n. 307;
M. Heiremans, 1993, n. 191;
M. Barovier, R. Barovier Mentasti,
A. Dorigato, 1995, n. 15;
Gli Artisti..., 1996, n. 1;
Il vetro italiano..., 1998, n. 25.

Trasparenti glass pieces by V.S.M.Cappellin Venini & C.; photo from the archives.

9. Vittorio Zecchin,
V.S.M. Cappellin Venini & C.

Trasparenti, 1921-1925

Vase in thin light blue ribbed transparent glass, decorated with two rings at the base of the neck. *Veronese* vase in thin amethyst-colored ribbed transparent glass. Vase in thin light blue transparent glass, ribbed and decorated with teardrop-shaped applications.
10.5" high (cm. 26); 10" high (cm. 25); 15.25" high (cm. 45)

Bibliography and comparative texts:
Mille anni..., 1982, n. 502;
F. Deboni, 1989, n. 4;
M. Barovier, 1999, p. 105.

Trasparenti glass pieces by V.S.M. Cappellin Venini & C., photo from the archives.

10. Vittorio Zecchin,
V.S.M. Cappellin Venini & C.

Trasparente, 1921-1925

A thin light blue transparent glass vase with applied handles. After the closing of the Cappellin Venini, the style was added to the catalogue of the M.V.M. Cappellin & C. as catalogue number 5293.
17" high (cm. 43)

Display of Cappellin Venini & C. at the first Esposizione Internazionale delle Arti Decorative, Monza, 1923.

11. Vittorio Zecchin,
V.S.M. Cappellin Venini & C.

Libellula, 1921-1925

Libellula (dragonfly) vessel in thin
blue transparent glass. This vessel is
characterized by two large handles, to
which it owes its name. After the 1925
closing of Cappellin Venini, the model
was included in both the M.V.M.
Cappellin & C. (n. 5481) and the V.S.M.
Venini & C. (n. 1432) catalogues.
Acid stamped: *M.V.M. Cappellin
Murano.*
7" high (cm. 18)

Exhibitions:
1923, Monza, 1st Esposizione
Internazionale delle Arti Decorative;
1924, Venice, 14th Biennale
Internazionale d'Arte (?).

Bibliography and comparative texts:
C. Carrà, 1923, p. 67;
R. Linzeler, 1923, p. 84;
R. Papini, 1923;
R. Barovier Mentasti, 1982, n. 253;
Mille anni..., 1982, n. 501;
W. Neuwirth, 1987, n. 110;
F. Deboni, 1989, p. 35;
L'arte del vetro..., 1992, n. 306;
M. Heiremans, 1993, n. 192;

M. Barovier, R. Barovier Mentasti,
A. Dorigato, 1995, n. 15;
M. Barovier, 1999, p. 104.

12. Napoleone Martinuzzi
V.S.M. Venini & C.

Trasparente, 1927 ca.

Large vase in transparent
green glass.
Acid stamped:
venini murano ITALIA and paper
label: n. 137.
17" high (cm. 44)

Bibliography and comparative texts:
W. Neuwirth, 1987, n. 6.

13. Napoleone Martinuzzi
V.S.M. Venini & C.

Pulegoso, 1930

Ten-handled vase in green
pulegoso glass. The handles and
mouth of the vase are decorated
with gold leaf applications. A similar
model was part of the collection of
the poet Gabriele d'Annunzio, now
on exhibition in the Stanza della
Zambracca at the Il Vittoriale degli
Italiani on Lake Garda.
13" high (cm. 34)

Exhibitions:
1930, Venice, 17th Biennale
Internazionale d'Arte;
1930, Monza, 4th Esposizione
Internazionale delle Arti Decorative
e Industriali Moderne.

Bibliography and comparative texts:
Venini blue catalogue, n. 3273:
photo n. 431, Triennale archives;
C.A. Felice, 1931, p. 64;
G. Lorenzetti, 1931;
Vetri Murano..., 1981, p. 30;
Mille anni..., 1982, n. 525;
R. Bossaglia, M. Quesada, 1988,
n. 338a;

F. Deboni, 1989, n. 14;
G. Duplani Tucci, 1989, n. 11;
M. Barovier, 1992, n. 80;
L'arte del vetro, 1992, n. 327;
F. Deboni, 1996, n. 180;
Gli Artisti..., 1996, n. 20;
Il vetro Italiano..., 1998, n. 38;
M. Barovier, 1999, p. 159.

Vases in *pulegoso* glass, published
in the January, 1931 issue of *Domus*.

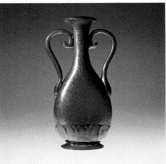

14. Napoleone Martinuzzi
V.S.M. Venini & C.

Pulegoso, 1930

Amphora in green *pulegoso* glass
with two large handles and ribbing
at the base.
18" high (cm. 46)

Exhibitions:
1930, Venice, 17th Biennale
Internazionale d'Arte;
1930, Monza, 4th Esposizione
Internazionale delle Arti Decorative
e Industriali Moderne.

Bibliography and comparative texts:
The Venetians..., 1989, n. 2;
Gli Artisti..., 1996, n. 25.

15. Napoleone Martinuzzi
Zecchin-Martinuzzi Vetri Artistici &
Mosaici

Incamiciato, 1932

Vase in *lattimo* glass cased in
turquoise glass with two handles
and foot decorated with applications
of gold leaf.
13.5" high (cm. 34)

Bibliography and comparative texts:
Mille anni..., 1982, n. 541;
M. Barovier, 1992, nn. 62, 63.

16. Napoleone Martinuzzi
Zecchin-Martinuzzi Vetri Artistici & Mosaici

Pasta Vitrea, 1933

Coral red footed vase composed of *pasta vitrea* with a twisted side handle.
Paper label: *Pauly & C.*
Pauly & C., a Venetian retail showroom, always affixed its own label to the Muranese glass it sold.
12" high (cm. 30)

Bibliography and comparative texts:
M. Barovier, 1992, n. 40.

Drawing from the Zecchin-Martinuzzi catalogue, 1933 ca.

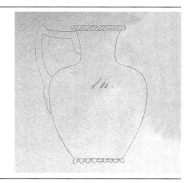

17. Carlo Scarpa
M.V.M. Cappellin & C.

Trasparente, 1926 - 1931

A straw-colored bowl composed of thin glass decorated with large bubbles. Foot and trim in red *pasta vitrea* with application of gold leaf.
Acid stamped: *M.V.M. Cappellin Murano.*
6.5" high (cm. 17)
8" Ø (cm. 20)

Drawing from M.V.M. Cappellin catalogue, 1930 ca.

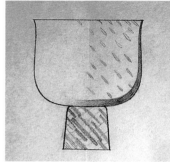

18. Carlo Scarpa
M.V.M. Cappellin & C.

Trasparente, 1926 - 1931

Light green globular-shaped vase in blown glass with a conical foot and mouth in blue glass.
This vase became the symbol of the M.V.M. Cappellin workshop.
5.5" high (cm. 14)

Exhibitions:
1926, Paris, Salon d'Automne;
1927, Monza, 3rd Mostra Internazionale delle Arti Decorative;
1930, Monza, 4th Mostra Internazionale delle Arti Decorative ed Industriali Moderne;
1931, Amsterdam, Exhibition of Modern Italian Art Glass, Ceramic and Lace.

Bibliography and comparative texts:
P. du Colombier, 1926, p. 187;
Domus, 1928, December, p. 59;
G. Dell'Oro, 1931, p. 563;
Mostra di vetri..., 1931, p. 19;

Domus, 1933, October, pp. 527, 528, 529;
R. Barovier Mentasti, 1982, p. 260;
Mille anni..., 1982, p. 262;
Vetri Murano..., 1982, p. 26;
Vetri di Murano..., 1982, n. 106;
F. Deboni, 1996, p. 34;
M. Barovier, 1997, p. 192;
M. Barovier, 1998b, p. 6;
M. Barovier, 1999, p. 114.

Interior of M.V.M. showroom in Florence, 1928 ca.

19. Carlo Scarpa
M.V.M. Cappellin & C.

Pasta vitrea, 1929 - 1930

A red *pasta vitrea* vase with two side handles, decorated throughout with gold leaf.
6" high (cm. 15)

Exhibitions:
1929, Paris, Salon d'Automne;
1930, Monza, 4th Esposizione delle Arti Decorative e Industriali Moderne;
1931, Amsterdam, Exhibition of Moderne Italian Art Glass, Ceramic and Lace;
1964, Venice, 32nd Biennale Internazionale d'Arte, Exhibition of the Decorative Arts of the Venetian Territory.

Bibliography and comparative texts:
M.V.M. Catalogue, n. 5911;
Domus, 1930, January, p. 38;
Mostra di vetri..., 1931, pp. 22, 23;

Venezianisches Glas...,1981, p. 64;
Vetro di Murano..., 1982, n. 122;
Mostra del Vetro..., 1984, p. 83;
The Venetians..., 1989, n. 4;
M. Barovier, 1991, n. 1, 2;
M. Barovier, 1997, p. 194;
M. Barovier, 1998b, pp. 7, 8, 9;
M. Barovier, 1999, p. 141.

Vessels in *pasta vitrea*, published in the January, 1930 issue of *Domus*.

20. Carlo Scarpa
M.V.M. Cappellin & C.

Trasparente a ballotton, 1930-1931
Incamiciato, 1929 - 1930

A globular-shaped vase in transparent green glass decorated a *ballotton* with gold leaf applications.
A globular-shaped vase in *lattimo* glass cased in red with a conical foot.
8" high (cm. 20),
6.75" high (cm. 17)

Exhibitions:
Incamiciato: 1930, Monza, 4th Esposizione delle Arti Decorative e Industriali Moderne;
1931, Amsterdam, Exhibition of Modern Italian Art Glass, Ceramic and Lace.

Bibliography and comparative texts:
Trasparente: M.V.M. Catalogue, n. 5673
Incamiciato: M.V.M. Catalogue, n. 5680
Dedalo, 1930, fasc.V, p. 321;
Domus, 1930, July, p. 41;
Domus, 1930, September, p. 32;

C.A. Felice, 1930, nn. 12, 30, 40, 81, 82;
U. Nebbia, 1930, p. 13;
Mostra di vetri..., 1931, pp. 22, 25, 26;
C.A. Felice, 1941, p. 81;
Vetri Murano..., 1981, p. 33;
Vetri di Murano..., 1982, n. 125;
Mostra del Vetro..., 1984, pp. 81, 84;
F. Deboni, 1996, n. 70;
M. Barovier, 1997, pp. 198, 199;
M. Barovier, 1998b, pp. 12, 13;
M. Barovier, 1999, p. 141.

Drawing from M.V.M. catalogue, 1930 ca.

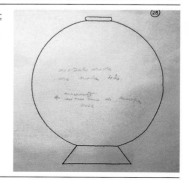

21. Carlo Scarpa
M.V.M. Cappellin & C.

Pasta vitrea, 1929-1930

A red *pasta vitrea* vase with applied foot.
Acid stamped: *M.V.M. Cappellin Murano.*
8.25" high (cm. 21)

Exhibitions:
1929, Paris, Salon d'Automne;
1930, Monza, 4th Esposizione delle Arti Decorative e Industriali Moderne;
1931, Amsterdam, Exhibition of Modern Italian Art Glass, Ceramic and Lace; 1964, Venice, 32nd Biennale Internazionale d'Arte, Exhibition of the Decorative Arts of the Venetian Territory.

Bibliography and comparative texts:
M.V.M. Catalogue, n. 5911;
Domus, 1930, January p. 38;
Mostra di vetri..., 1931, pp. 22, 23;
Venezianisches Glas..., 1981, p. 64;

Vetro di Murano..., 1982, n. 122;
Mostra del vetro..., 1984, p. 83;
The Venetians..., 1989, n. 4;
M. Barovier, 1991, nn. 1, 2;
M. Barovier, 1997, p. 194;
M. Barovier, 1998b, pp. 7, 8, 9;
M. Barovier, 1999, p. 141.

Vessels in *pasta vitrea*; photo from M.V.M. archives, 1930 ca.

22. Carlo Scarpa
M.V.M. Cappellin & C.

Pasta vitrea, 1930

Red iridized *pasta vitrea* pitcher with a large handle and trim in black *pasta vitrea*.
Acid stamped:
M.V.M. Cappellin Murano.
12" high (cm. 30)

Exhibitions:
1929, Paris, Salon d'Automne;
1930, Monza, 4th Esposizione delle Arti Decorative e Industriali Moderne;
1931, Amsterdam, Exhibition of Modern Italian Art Glass, Ceramic and Lace; 1964, Venice, 32nd Biennale Internazionale d'Arte, Exhibition of the Decorative Arts of the Venetian Territory.

Bibliography and comparative texts:
M.V.M. Catalogue, n. 5536;
Domus, 1930, January p. 38;
Mostra di vetri..., 1931, pp. 22, 23;
Venezianisches Glas..., 1981, p. 64;

Vetro di Murano..., 1982, n. 122;
Mostra del vetro..., 1984, p. 83;
The venetians..., 1989, n. 4;
M. Barovier, 1991, nn. 1, 2;
M. Barovier, 1997, p. 194;
M. Barovier, 1998b, pp. 7, 8, 9;
M. Barovier, 1999, p. 141.

23. Carlo Scarpa
M.V.M. Cappellin & C.

Fenicio, 1928-1929

Globular-shaped vase in *lattimo* glass with red *decoro fenicio* in *pasta vitrea* and gold leaf applications.
5.5" high (cm. 13)

Exhibitions:
1964, Venice, 32nd Biennale Internazionale d'Arte, Exhibition of the Decorative Arts of the Venetian Territory.

Bibliography and comparative texts:
M.V.M. Catalogue, n. 5934;
Domus, 1930, January, p. 38;
M. Barovier, 1991, nn. 3, 4;
R. Barovier Mentasti, 1992, n. 62;
L'arte del vetro..., 1992, p. 243;
H. Newman 1993, p. 145;
Glas Band II, 1995, p. 232;
M. Heiremans, 1996, n. 32;
F. Deboni, 1996, n. 66;

M. Barovier, 1997, p. 195;
M. Barovier, 1998b, pp. 8, 9.

Fenici vases, photo from the M.V.M. Cappellin archives, 1930 ca.

24. Carlo Scarpa
M.V.M. Cappellin & C.

Fenicio, 1930-1931

Lattimo vase cased in transparent straw-colored glass with blue *decoro fenicio*.
Acid stamped:
M.V.M. Cappellin Murano.
6.5" high (cm. 17)

Exhibitions:
1964, Venice, 32nd Biennale Internazionale d'Arte, Exhibition of the Decorative Arts of the Venetian Territory.

Bibliography and comparative texts:
Domus, 1930, January, p. 38;
M. Barovier, 1991, nn. 3, 4;
R. Barovier Mentasti, 1992, n. 62;
L'arte del vetro..., 1992, p. 243;
H. Newman, 1993, p. 145;
Glas Band II, 1995, p. 232;
M. Heiremans, 1996, n. 32;
F. Deboni, 1996, n. 66;
M. Barovier, 1997, p. 195;

M. Barovier, 1998b, pp. 8, 9.

25. Carlo Scarpa
M.V.M. Cappellin & C.

Pasta vitrea, 1929-1930
Fenicio, 1928-1931

A green *pasta vitrea* vase. A black *pasta vitrea* globular vase with a green *fenicio* decoration on a conic foot. Both vases decorated with gold leaf applications.
Both acid stamped: *M.V.M. Cappellin Murano.*
6.5" high (cm. 16);
6.75" high (cm. 17)

Exhibitions:
1964, Venice, 32nd Biennale Internazionale d'Arte, Exhibition of the Decorative Arts of the Venetian Territory.

Bibliography and comparative texts:
M.V.M. Catalogue, n. 5911;
Domus, 1930, January, p. 38;
Mostra di vetri..., 1931, pp. 22, 23;
Venezianisches Glas..., 1981, p. 64;
Vetro di Murano..., 1982, n. 122;
Mostra del vetro..., 1984, p. 83;
The Venetians..., 1989, n. 4;
M. Barovier, 1991, nn. 1, 2;
M. Barovier, 1997, p. 194;

M. Barovier, 1998b, pp. 7, 8, 9;
M. Barovier, 1999, p. 141.
Fenici: see description n. 23

Vases in *pasta vitrea*; photo from the M.V.M. Cappellin archives, 1930 ca.

26. Carlo Scarpa
M.V.M. Cappellin & C.

Millefiori, 1930-1931
Fenici, 1928-1931

A *millefiori* footed bowl cased in light blue *lattimo* glass with inclusions of circular light blue *murrine. Decoro fenicio* vases, one cased in pink *lattimo* glass, the other cased in light blue glass. Pink and blue trim.
Acid stamped: *M.V.M. Cappellin Murano.*
8" high (cm. 20); 8" high (cm. 20); 10.5" high (cm. 26.5)

Exhibitions:
Millefiori: 1930, Monza, 4th Esposizione Internazionale delle Arti Decorative e Industriali Moderne;
1931, Amsterdam, Exhibition of Modern Italian Art Glass, Ceramic and Lace.
Fenici: see description n. 23.

Bibliography and comparative texts:
Millefiori: M.V.M. Catalogue, n. 5821;
C.A. Felice 1930, n. 12;
Mostra di vetri..., 1931, p. 25;
M. Barovier, 1991, n. 10
R. Barovier Mentasti, 1992, n. 66;
L'arte del vetro..., 1992, p. 241;

M. Heiremans, 1993, n. 87;
F. Deboni, 1996 n. 67;
M. Heiremans, 1996, n. 36;
M. Barovier, 1997, pp. 200, 201;
M. Barovier, 1998b, p. 14;
M. Barovier, 1999, p. 141.
Fenici: see description n. 23.

27. Carlo Scarpa
M.V.M. Cappellin & C.

Iridato, 1929-1931

A black iridized glass plate with a spiral decor in *lattimo* glass
Acid stamped: *M.V.M. Cappellin Murano.*
9.5" Ø (cm. 24)

Bibliography and comparative texts:
Vetri di Murano..., 1982, n. 118;
M. Barovier, 1997, n. 83, p. 197;
M. Barovier, 1998b, p. 11.

28. Carlo Scarpa
M.V.M. Cappellin & C.

Lattimo, 1929

Lattimo glass amphora with two handles, decorated with oxidized gold leaf applications over the entire surface.
9.5" high (cm. 24)

Exhibitions:
1930, Monza, 4th Esposizione Internazionale delle Arti Decorative e Industriali Moderne;
1931, Amsterdam, Exhibition of Modern Italian Art Glass, Ceramic and Lace.

Bibliography and comparative texts:
Artisti italiani..., 1929;
Domus, 1929, April, p. 35;
Domus, 1929, October, pp. 30, 31;
Domus, 1930, January, p. 39;
Mostra di vetri..., 1931, p. 21;
The Venetians..., 1989, n.1;
M. Barovier, 1991, nn. 5, 6, pp. 51, 53;

M. Heiremans, 1993, n. 77;
F. Deboni, 1996 n. 63;
M. Heiremans, 1996, n. 25;
M. Barovier, 1997, pp. 196, 197;
M. Barovier, 1998b, pp. 10, 11;
M. Barovier, 1999, p. 141.

29. Carlo Scarpa
M.V.M. Cappellin & C.

Lattimo, 1929

Globular *lattimo* glass vase with oxidized gold leaf applications.
Rim around the mouth in red *pasta vitrea.*
5.25" high (cm. 13)

Exhibitions:
1930, Monza, 4th Esposizione Internazionale delle Arti Decorative e Industriali Moderne;
1931, Amsterdam, Exhibition of Modern Italian Art Glass, Ceramic and Lace.

Bibliography and comparative texts:
M.V.M. Catalogue, n. 5932;
Artisti italiani..., 1929;
Domus, 1929, April, p. 35;
Domus, 1929, October, p. 30, 31;
Domus, 1930, January, p. 39;
Mostra di vetri..., 1931, p. 21;
The Venetians..., 1989, n. 1;

M. Barovier, 1991, nn. 5, 6, pp. 51, 53;
M. Heiremans, 1993, n. 77;
F. Deboni, 1996, n. 63;
M. Heiremans, 1996, n. 25;
M. Barovier, 1997, pp. 196, 197;
M. Barovier, 1998b, pp. 10, 11;
M. Barovier, 1999, p. 141.

Vase in *lattimo* glass published in the April 1929 issue of *Domus*.

30. Carlo Scarpa
M.V.M. Cappellin & C.

Lattimi, 1929-1930

Two vases in *lattimo* glass with applications of oxidized gold and silver leaf.
6.75" high (cm. 17);
9" high (cm. 23)

Exhibitions:
1930, Monza, 4th Esposizione Internazionale delle Arti Decorative e Industriali Moderne;
1931, Amsterdam, Exhibition of Modern Italian Art Glass, Ceramic and Lace.

Bibliography and comparative texts:
M.V.M. Catalogue, n. 6015;
Artisti italiani..., 1929;
Domus, 1929, April, p. 35;
Domus, 1929, October, p. 30, 31;
Domus, 1930, January, p. 39;
Mostra di vetri..., 1931, p. 21;
The Venetians..., 1989, n. 1;

M. Barovier, 1991, nn. 5, 6, pp. 51, 53;
M. Heiremans, 1993, n. 77;
F. Deboni, 1996 n. 63;
M. Heiremans, 1996, n. 25;
M. Barovier, 1997, pp. 196, 197;
M. Barovier, 1998b, pp. 10, 11;
M. Barovier, 1999, p. 141.

31. Carlo Scarpa
M.V.M. Cappellin & C.

Incamiciati, 1930

Red *pasta vitrea* footed bowl with handles and hexagonal vase in red *pasta vitrea* cased in purple glass, both with applied oxidized silver leaf.
3.5" high (cm. 9);
12" high (cm. 30)

Exhibitions:
1930, Monza, 4th Esposizione Internazionale delle Arti Decorative e Industriali Moderne;
1931, Amsterdam, Exhibition of Modern Italian Art Glass, Ceramic and Lace.

Bibliography and comparative texts:
Vessel: M.V.M. Catalogue, n. 5992;
Dedalo, 1930, fasc. V, p. 321;
Domus, 1930, July, p. 41;
Domus, 1930, September, p. 32;
C.A. Felice, 1930, nn. 12, 30, 40;
U. Nebbia, 1930, p. 13;
R. Pacini, 1930, p. 273;

C.A. Felice, 1941, p. 81;
Vetri Murano..., 1981, p. 33;
Vetri di Murano..., 1982, n. 125;
Mostra del vetro..., 1984, pp. 81, 84;
M. Heiremans, 1996, nn. 85, 86;
F. Deboni, 1996, nn. 70, 71;
M. Barovier, 1997, pp. 198, 199;
M. Barovier, 1998b, pp. 12, 13.

Vessels in *incamiciato* glass in the Catalogue of the Exhibition of Modern Italian Art Glass, Ceramics and Lace, Amsterdam, 1931.

32. Carlo Scarpa
M.V.M. Cappellin & C.

Incamiciato, 1930

A large footed vase decorated with a shell in *lattimo* glass, cased in amethyst-colored glass. The shell and trim in red *pasta vitrea*. Light applications of gold leaf over the entire surface.
11" high (cm. 28)

Exhibitions:
1930, Monza, 4th Esposizione Internazionale delle Arti Decorative e Industriali Moderne;
1931, Amsterdam, Exhibition of Modern Italian Art Glass, Ceramic and Lace; 1964, Venice, 32nd Biennale Internazionale d'Arte, Exhibition of the Decorative Arts of the Venetian Territory.

Bibliography and comparative texts:
Dedalo, 1930, fasc. V, p. 321;
Domus, 1930, July, p. 41;
Domus, 1930, September, p. 32;
C.A. Felice, 1930, nn. 12, 30, 40, 81, 82;

U. Nebbia, 1930, p. 13;
R. Pacini, 1930, p. 273;
Mostra di Vetri..., 1931, pp. 22, 25, 26;
C.A. Felice, 1941, p. 81;
Vetri Murano..., 1981, p. 33;
Vetri di Murano..., 1982, n. 125;
Mostra del vetro..., 1984, pp. 81, 84;
M. Heiremans, 1996, nn. 85, 86;
F. Deboni, 1996, nn. 70, 71;
M. Barovier, 1997, pp. 198, 199;
M. Barovier, 1998b, pp. 12, 13;
M. Barovier, 1999, p. 141.

33. Tomaso Buzzi
V.S.M. Venini & C.

Turchese e nero, 1932

A turquoise glass bowl with a black conic foot and an applied outlined fish. Fish decor and trim in black glass.
Paper label: *Vetri Soffiati Muranesi Venini & C.*
4.75" high (cm. 12)

Exhibitions:
1932, Venice, 18th Biennale Internazionale d'Arte.

Bibliography and comparative texts:
P. Chiesa, 1932, p. 417;
F. Deboni, 1989, n. 36;
M. Barovier, R. Barovier Mentasti, A. Dorigato, 1995, n. 28;
F. Deboni, 1996, p. 73;
Gli Artisti..., 1996, n. 51.

The Venini display at the 18th Biennale Internazionale d'Arte, Venice, 1932.

34. Tomaso Buzzi
V.S.M. Venini & C.

Alga, 1933

Footed bowl in *alga* glass, cased with several layers of colored glass, *incamiciato*. Applied *lattimo* glass foot. Gold leaf applications over the entire surface.
2.25" high (cm. 6)

Exhibitions:
1933, Milan, 5th Triennale.

Bibliography and comparative texts:
Venini blue catalogue, n. 1781;
Domus, 1933, February, p. 83;
R. Papini, 1933, p. 870;
F. Deboni, 1989, n. 41;
M. Heiremans, 1993, n. 194;
Gli Artisti..., 1996, n. 53, 55;
Il vetro italiano..., 1998, nn. 52, 53.

35. Tomaso Buzzi
V.S.M. Venini & C.

Alba, 1933

A footed pitcher in light blue *alba* glass, cased with several layers of colored glass, *incamiciato*. Heart-shaped mouth. Foot and prunted collar in *cristallo* glass. The whole pitcher decorated with gold leaf applications.
6.75" high (cm. 17)

Exhibitions:
1933, Milan, 5th Triennale.

Bibliography and comparative texts:
Venini blue catalogue, n. 3464;
R. Aloi, 1955 p. 27;
Mille anni..., 1982, n. 527;
F. Deboni, 1989, n. 38;
R. Barovier Mentasti 1992, n. 57;
Gli Artisti..., 1996, n. 52, 54;
M. Barovier, 1999, p. 161.
Il vetro italiano..., 1998, nn. 52, 53, 54.

Vessels in *incamiciato* glass with several layers of color; photo from the Venini archives, 1933 ca.

36. Tomaso Buzzi
V.S.M. Venini & C.

Laguna, 1933

Footed vase in pink *laguna* glass cased with several layers of colored glass, *incamiciato*. Foot in *lattimo* glass. Gold leaf application over the entire surface.
8" high (cm. 20)

Exhibitions:
1933, Milan, 5th Triennale.

Bibliography and comparative texts:
Venini blue catalogue, n. 3450;
Domus, 1933, February, p. 82;
R. Papini, 1933, p. 870;
F. Deboni, 1989, nn. 35, 45;
L'arte del vetro..., 1991, n. 17;
M. Heiremans, 1993, n. 194;
Gli Artisti..., 1996, nn. 52, 57.

Venini display case at the 5th Triennale, Milan, 1933.

37. Tomaso Buzzi
V.S.M. Venini & C.

Incamiciato, 1932

Lattimo glass flask cased in straw-colored glass. Applied handles. Gold leaf applications throughout. Acid stamped: *venini murano*.
7" high (cm. 18)

Bibliography and comparative texts:
La metafisica..., 1980, p. 242.

38. Carlo Scarpa
Venini & C.

A bollicine, 1932-1934

Iridized green glass bowl, composed of densely bubbled *a bollicine* glass.
4.5" high (cm. 11)

Bibliography and comparative texts:
G. Ponti, 1959, p. 35;
The Venetians..., 1989, n. 10;
F. Deboni, 1989, n. 46;
M. Heiremans, 1993, n. 197;
Glas Band II, 1995, p. 227;
M. Barovier, R. Barovier Mentasti,
A. Dorigato, 1995, p. 76;
Gli Artisti..., 1996, nn. 68, 72;
Italienisches..., 1996, n. 22;
M. Barovier, 1997, p. 204;
M. Barovier, 1998b, p. 18;
M. Barovier, 1999, p. 167.

39. Carlo Scarpa
Venini & C.

A bollicine, 1932-1936

A blue, strongly iridized footed vase composed of densely bubbled *a bollicine* glass. A green vase composed of densely bubbled *a bollicine* glass with inclusions of red star-shaped *murrine*. The blue vase is acid stamped: *venini murano*.
9" high (cm. 23)
4.5" high (cm. 11)

Bibliography and comparative texts:
Venini blue catalogue, n. 11030;
G. Ponti, 1959, p. 35;
The Venetians..., 1989, n. 10;
F. Deboni, 1989, n. 46;
M. Heiremans, 1993, n. 197;
Glas Band II, 1995, p. 227;
M. Barovier, R. Barovier Mentasti,
A. Dorigato, 1995, p. 76;
Gli Artisti..., 1996, nn. 68, 72;
Italienisches..., 1996, n. 22;
M. Barovier, 1997, p. 204;
M. Barovier, 1998b, p. 18;
M. Barovier, 1999, p. 167.

40. Carlo Scarpa
Venini & C.

A bollicine, 1934-1936

One green vase with squared top *a bollicine* glass. One stoppered white footed vase *a bollicine* glass. One green globular footed vase *a bollicine* glass. Unsigned, acid stamped *venini murano MADE IN ITALY* and *venini murano*.
7" high (cm. 18)
9.5" high (cm. 24)
8.75" high (cm. 22)

Bibliography and comparative texts:
Venini blue catalogue, nn. 431, 11012;
G. Ponti, 1959, p. 35;
The Venetians..., 1989, n. 10;
F. Deboni, 1989, n. 46;
M. Heiremans, 1993, n. 197;
Glas Band II, 1995, p. 227;
M. Barovier, R. Barovier Mentasti,
A. Dorigato, 1995, p. 76;
Gli Artisti..., 1996, nn. 68, 72;
Italienisches..., 1996, n. 22;
M. Barovier, 1997, p. 204;
M. Barovier, 1998b, p. 18;
M. Barovier, 1999, p. 167.

41. Carlo Scarpa
Venini & C.

Sommerso a bollicine, 1934-1936

Vase in yellow *sommerso a bollicine* glass with inclusion of gold leaf. Acid stamped: *venini murano*.
8" high (cm. 20)

Exhibitions:
1934, Venice, 19th Biennale Internazionale d'Arte;
1936, Venice, 20th Biennale Internazionale d'Arte;
1936, Milan, 6th Triennale.

Bibliography and comparative texts:
Venini blue catalogue, n. 3507.
In addition, see description n. 42.

Vessels in *sommerso* glass published in the July 1936 issue of *Domus*.

42. Carlo Scarpa
Venini & C.

Sommersi a bollicine, 1934-1936

Vases in *sommerso a bollicine* glass with inclusions of gold leaf: one in green *sommerso a bollicine*, one in amethyst with controlled air bubbles, and the third in light blue *a bollicine* glass with an applied foot in *cristallo*. Acid stamped: *venini murano*.
8.75" high (cm. 22)
5" high (cm. 13)
10.5" high (cm. 27)

Exhibitions:
1934, Venice, 19th Biennale Internazionale d'Arte; 1936, Venice, 20th Biennale Internazionale d'Arte; 1936, Milan, 6th Triennale.

Bibliography and comparative texts:
Venini blue catalogue, n. 3194, n. 352, n. 11011; *Domus*, 1934, September, p. 34; *Domus*, 1934, November, p. 23; E. Motta, 1934, p. 275; G. Dell'Oro, 1935, p. 30; *Le Tre Venezie*, 1936, August/September, p. 268; G. Ponti, 1936, p. 31; *Domus*, 1939, February, p. 61; R. Aloi, 1955, p. 12;

G. Ponti, 1959, p. 35; *Carlo Scarpa...*, 1984, p. 185; *Mostra del Vetro...*,1984, p. 112; F. Deboni, 1989, nn. 47, 48; M. Barovier, 1991, n. 13; M. Barovier, R. Barovier Mentasti, A. Dorigato, 1995, nn. 36, 37; *Gli Artisti...*, 1996, nn. 69, 70, 71, 73-81; *Italienisches...*, 1996, nn. 20, 21; M. Barovier, 1997, pp. 205, 206; M. Barovier, 1998b, p. 20; *Il vetro italiano...*, 1998, n. 71; M. Barovier, 1999, pp. 165, 167.

Vessels in *sommerso* glass published in the September 1934 issue of *Domus*.

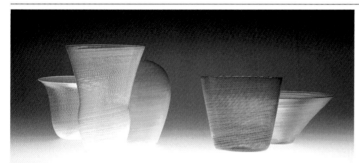

43. Carlo Scarpa
Venini & C.

Mezza filigrana, 1934-1936

Vases in *a mezza filigrana* glass: one light blue, one white, one green and two red/orange glass. The outer vases acid stamped: *venini murano* and the three middle vases stamped *venini murano MADE IN ITALY*.
6" high (cm. 15)
9" high (cm. 23)
8" high (cm. 20)
6.75" high (cm. 17)
4.75" high (cm. 12)

Exhibitions:
1934, Venice, 19th Biennale Internazionale d'Arte; 1936, Venice, 20th Biennale Internazionale d'Arte; 1936, Milan, 6th Triennale.

Bibliography and comparative texts:
Venini blue catalogue, nn. 3908, 3507, 3517, 3518; *Domus*, 1934, September p. 35; *Domus*, 1934, November, p. 25; E. Motta, 1934, p. 276; C.A. Felice, 1936, p. 25; *Domus*, 1938, December, p. 28; G. Mariacher, 1954, p. 156; R. Aloi, 1955, p. 12;

G. Ponti, 1959, p. 40; M. Brusatin, 1972, p. 23; *Space Design*, 1977, p. 69; *Carlo Scarpa...*, 1984, p. 184; F. Deboni, 1989, n. 45; M. Barovier, 1991, n. 11; *Vetri veneziani del '900*, 1994, p. 47; M. Barovier, R. Barovier Mentasti, A. Dorigato, 1995, n. 35; *Glas Band II*, 1995, p. 228; *Gli Artisti...*, 1996, nn. 65, 66; *Italienisches...*, 1996, nn. 23, 24; M. Barovier, 1997, pp. 206, 207; M. Barovier, 1999, p. 167.

44. Carlo Scarpa
Venini & C.

Mezza filigrana, 1934-1936

A red *a mezza filigrana* vase *sommerso in cristallo*. Acid stamped: *venini murano*.
7.5" high (cm. 19)

Bibliography and comparative texts:
Domus, 1934, September p. 35; *Domus*, 1934, November, p. 25; E. Motta, 1934, p. 276; C.A. Felice, 1936, p. 25; *Domus*, 1938, December, p. 28; G. Mariacher, 1954, p. 156; R. Aloi, 1955, p.12; G. Ponti, 1959, p.40; M. Brusatin, 1972, p. 23; *Space Design*, 1977, p. 69; *Carlo Scarpa...*, 1984, p. 184; F. Deboni, 1989, n. 45; M. Barovier, 1991, n. 11; *Vetri veneziani del '900*, 1994, p. 47; M. Barovier, R. Barovier Mentasti,

A. Dorigato, 1995, n. 35; *Glas Band II*, 1995, p. 228; *Gli Artisti...*, 1996, nn. 65, 66; *Italienisches...*, 1996, nn. 23, 24; M. Barovier, 1997, pp. 206, 207; M. Barovier, 1999, p. 167.

Vessels in *a mezza filigrana* glass published in *Arti industriali oggi*, 1936.

45. Carlo Scarpa,
Venini & C.

Lattimo, 1934-1936

Vase in *lattimo* glass. Acid stamped: *venini murano MADE IN ITALY*.
9.5" high (cm. 24)

Exhibitions:
1936, Venice, 20th Biennale Internazionale d'Arte;
1936, Milan, 6th Triennale.

Bibliography and comparative texts:
Venini blue catalogue, n. 3579; C.A. Felice, 1936, pp. 24, 26; M. Barovier, R. Barovier Mentasti, A. Dorigato, 1995, n. 42; *Italienisches...*, 1996, n. 18; M. Barovier, 1997, p. 210, 211; M. Barovier, 1997, p. 209; M. Barovier, 1998b, p. 24.

Venini display at the 6th Triennale, Milan, 1936.

46. Carlo Scarpa
Venini & C.

Corrosi, 1936

Vase in straw-colored *corroso* glass with applied spiraling *fasce*.
Vase in green *corroso* glass with applied *bugne*. Both vases finished with an iridescent surface.
Acid stamped: *venini murano*.
12.5" high (cm. 32)
8" high (cm. 20)

Exhibitions:
1936, Venice, 20th Biennale Internazionale d'Arte;
1936, Milan, 6th Triennale.

Bibliography and comparative texts:
Venini blue catalogue, nn. 4103, 4101;
G. Dell'Oro, 1936, p. 272;
Domus, 1936, December, p. 37;
C.A. Felice, 1936, pp. 26, 27, 29;
Le Tre Venezie, 1936, July, p. 230;
G. Ponti, 1936, pp. 30, 31;
Domus, 1938, December, p. 33;
Domus, 1939, February, p. 56;
W. Neuwith, 1987, nn. 30, 31;
F. Deboni, 1989, nn. 49, 50, 51, 53;

M. Heiremans, 1993, nn. 203, 204;
M. Barovier, R. Barovier Mentasti, A. Dorigato, 1995, n. 43;
F. Deboni, 1996, n. 191;
M. Heiremans, 1996, nn. 48, 49;
Italienisches..., 1996, nn. 27, 29, 30, 31, 32; M. Barovier, 1997, pp. 210, 211; M. Barovier, 1998b, pp. 22-24;
Il vetro italiano..., 1998, nn. 72, 73;
M. Barovier, 1999, p. 167.

Vases in *corroso* glass published in the July 1936 issue of *Domus*.

47. Carlo Scarpa
Venini & C.

Corrosi, 1936

Vessels in *cristallo corroso* glass, both finished with an iridescent surface.
Acid stamped: *venini murano ITALIA*.
3" high (cm. 8)
4.5" high (cm. 11)

Exhibitions:
1936, Venice, 20th Biennale Internazionale d'Arte;
1936, Milan, 6th Triennale.

Bibliography and comparative texts:
Venini blue catalogue, nn. 4110, 4113;
G. Dell'Oro, 1936, p. 272;
Domus, 1936, December, p. 37;
C.A. Felice, 1936, pp. 26, 27, 29;
Le Tre Venezie, 1936, July, p. 230;
G. Ponti, 1936, pp. 30, 31;
Domus, 1938, December, p. 33;
Domus, 1939, February, p. 56;
W. Neuwirth, 1987, nn. 30, 31;
F. Deboni, 1989, nn. 49, 50, 51, 53;

M. Heiremans, 1993, nn. 203, 204;
M. Barovier, R. Barovier Mentasti, A. Dorigato, 1995, n. 43;
F. Deboni, 1996, n. 191;
M. Heiremans, 1996, nn. 48, 49;
Italienisches..., 1996, nn. 27, 29, 30, 31, 32;
M. Barovier, 1997, pp. 210, 211;
M. Barovier, 1998, pp. 22, 23, 24;
Vetro italiano..., 1998, nn. 72, 73;
M. Barovier, 1999, p. 167.

Venini display at the 6th Triennale, Milan, 1936.

48. Carlo Scarpa
Venini & C.

Murrine romane, 1936

Vase made of transparent *murrine*. The core of each *murrine* is composed of black glass.
This series was designed by Carlo Scarpa in collaboration with Paolo Venini.
4.5" high (cm. 10)

Exhibitions:
1936, Venice, 20th Biennale Internazionale d'Arte;
1936, Milan, 6th Triennale.

Bibliography and comparative texts:
Venini blue catalogue, n. 4007;
Domus, 1936, December, p. 37;
C.A. Felice, 1936, p. 24;
G. Ponti, 1936, p. 29;
R. Barovier Mentasti, 1992, n. 68;
M. Heiremans, 1993, n. 199;
M. Barovier, 1994, n. 13;
M. Barovier, R. Barovier Mentasti, A. Dorigato, 1995, n. 41;
F. Deboni, 1996, p. 73;

M. Barovier, 1997, p. 208;
M. Barovier, 1998b, p. 21;
M. Barovier, 1999, p. 167.

Vessels made of *murrine romane* published in *Arti industriali oggi*, 1936.

49. Carlo Scarpa
Venini & C.

Soffiato trasparente, 1936

Lightly iridized vase in thin straw-colored clear glass.
Acid stamped: *venini murano MADE IN ITALY*.
8.5" high (cm. 21)

Exhibitions:
1936, Venice, 20th Biennale Internazionale d'Arte;
1936, Milano, 6th Triennale.

Bibliography and comparative texts:
Venini blue catalogue, n. 3586;
Domus, 1934, December, p. 32;
C.A. Felice, 1936, pp. 23, 26, 29;
M. Barovier, R. Barovier Mentasti, A. Dorigato, 1995, n. 41;
M. Barovier, 1997, p. 208.

50. Carlo Scarpa
Venini & C.

A fasce, 1938

A clear glass vase decorated with a spiraling *fascia*, which is half in *lattimo* glass and half in red *pasta vitrea*.
Acid stamped: *venini murano MADE IN ITALY*.
9.5" high (cm. 24)

Exhibitions:
1938, Venice, 21st Biennale Internazionale d'Arte.

Bibliography and comparative texts:
Domus, 1936, July, p. 19.
Le Tre Venezie, 1938, June, p. 46.
M. Heiremans, 1996, n. 59.
M. Barovier, 1997, pp. 212, 213;
M. Barovier, 1998b, p. 25.

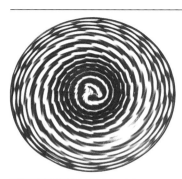

51. Carlo Scarpa
Venini & C.

Variegato zigrinato, 1938

Bowl in clear iridized glass
decorated with a spiral of red
pasta vitrea.
Acid stamped: *venini murano*.
9" Ø (cm. 23)

Exhibitions:
1938, Venice, 21st Biennale
Internazionale d'Arte.

Bibliography and comparative texts:
Le Tre Venezie, 1938, June, p. 247;
M. Heiremans, 1993, n. 206;
M. Barovier, 1997, p. 213;
M. Barovier, 1998b, p. 25;
M. Barovier, 1999, p. 167.

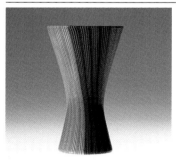

52. Carlo Scarpa
Venini & C.

Tessuto, 1940

A bi-colored vase, one half
composed of thin vertical canes
in red and black, the other in
red and *lattimo* canes.
Acid stamped: *venini murano*.
6.75" high (cm. 17)

Exhibitions:
1940, Venice, 22nd Biennale
Internazionale d'Arte.

Bibliography and comparative texts:
G. Ponti, 1940, p. 70;
G. Mariacher, 1954, p. 169;
R. Aloi, 1955, p. 27;
G. Ponti, 1959, p. 40;
R. Barovier Mentasti, 1977, n. 67;
Venezianisches..., 1981, p. 68;
Mille anni..., 1982, n. 529;
Vetro di Murano..., 1982, n. 144;
R. Barovier Mentasti, 1982, p. 284;
M. Miani, D. Resini, F. Lamon, 1984,
p. 84;

W. Neuwirth, 1987, p. 197;
F. Deboni, 1989, n. 68, 69, 70;
G. Duplani Tucci, 1989, nn. 17, 18;
H. Ricke, 1990, p. 234;
M. Barovier, 1991, n. 38, 39;
L'arte del vetro..., 1992, p. 253;
M. Heiremans, 1993, n. 202;
M. Barovier, 1994, n. 12;
M. Barovier, R. Barovier Mentasti,
A. Dorigato, 1995, n. 58;
H. Ricke, 1995, p.236;
Gli Artisti..., 1996, nn. 114, 115, 116;
M. Heiremans, 1996, n. 65;
Italienisches..., 1996, nn. 39, 40, 41;
M. Barovier, 1997, pp. 214, 215;
M. Barovier, 1998b, p. 25;

Il vetro italiano..., 1998, n. 90;
Venini Venezia, 1998, p. 67;
M. Barovier, 1999, p. 187.

53. Carlo Scarpa
Venini & C.

Tessuto, 1940

A vase composed of thin vertical
canes in green and amethyst,
sommerso in *cristallo*.
Acid stamped: *venini murano*.
8.75" high (cm. 22)

Bibliography and comparative texts:
Venini blue catalogue, n. 3594.
In addition, see description n. 52.

54. Carlo Scarpa
Venini & C.

Tessuto, 1940

A bi-colored *velato* finished vase,
one half composed of thin vertical
canes in amethyst and *lattimo*, the
other in yellow and *lattimo*.
Acid stamped: *venini murano MADE
IN ITALY*.
13.5" high (cm. 34.5)

Exhibitions:
1940, Venice, 22nd Biennale
Internazionale d'Arte.

Bibliography and comparative texts:
Venini grey catalogue, n. 4550.
In addition, see description n. 52.

Vases in *tessuto* glass at an
exhibition of Venini; photo from
the archives.

55. Carlo Scarpa
Venini & C.

Laccati rossi e neri, 1940

Vase and bowl in black and red a
incalmo glass. In this series, the red
glass was obtained by mixing small
particles of pre-finished glass into
the molten glass.
Acid stamped:
venini murano MADE IN ITALY and
venini murano ITALIA. Paper label.
6.75" high (cm. 17)
2.75" high (cm. 7)
9.5" Ø (cm. 24.5)

Exhibitions:
1940, Venice, 22nd Biennale
Internazionale d'Arte.

Bibliography and comparative texts:
Venini blue catalogue, nn. 3611, 3601;
C.A. Felice, 1941, pp. 54, 55;
F. Deboni, 1989, pp. 24, 27;
L'arte del vetro..., 1992, p. 251;
M. Barovier, R. Barovier Mentasti,
A. Dorigato, 1995, n. 55;
F. Deboni, 1996, p. 75;
Gli Artisti..., 1996 n. 97;
Italienisches..., 1996, n. 26;
M. Barovier, 1997, p. 216;
M. Barovier, 1998, p. 27.

56. Carlo Scarpa
per Venini & C., Murano

Granulare, 1940

A black bowl made of *murrine* with opaline core. The granular look was caused by the difference in the cooling times of the black and the opaline glass: the opaline glass solidified first, thus remaining in relief on the surface of the vessel.
Paper label: *Venini n. 4116*.
6" high (cm. 15)
8.5" Ø (cm. 21)

Exhibitions:
1940 Milano, 7th Triennale.

Bibliography and comparative texts:
G. Ponti, 1940, p. 60;
F. Deboni, 1989, n. 64;
M. Barovier, 1991, n. 42;
L'arte del vetro..., 1992, p. 250;
Gli Artisti..., 1996, n. 96;
M. Barovier, 1997, p. 216.

57. Carlo Scarpa
Venini & C.

Iridati, 1940

Two iridized bowls, one in green glass cased in amethyst, the other in amethyst cased in light blue. These objects are very thin and part of an extremely rare series. Depending on the angle of light to which they are exposed they transmit a different color.
Acid stamped: *venini murano*.
3.25" high (cm. 8) 4.75" Ø (cm. 12)
4.75" high (cm. 12) 8" Ø (cm. 20)

Exhibitions:
1940, Venice, 22nd Biennale Internazionale d'Arte;
1940, Milan, 7th Triennale.

Bibliography and comparative texts:
Venini blue catalogue, nn. 3920, 3767;
G. Ponti, 1940 a, p. 58;
G. Ponti, 1940 b, p. 71;
Lo Stile, 1941, p. 50;
Space Design, 1977, p. 70;
F. Deboni, 1989, pp. 27, 50;
M. Barovier, 1991, n. 34;
M. Barovier, R. Barovier Mentasti,
A. Dorigato, 1995, n. 60;
Gli Artisti..., 1996, n. 127;

M. Barovier, 1997, p. 217;
M. Barovier, 1998a, p. 27.

Vases in iridized glass, photo from the archives of the Triennale, 1940.

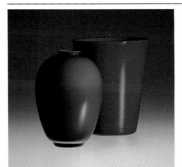

58. Carlo Scarpa
Venini & C.

Cinesi, 1940

Two vases, one in light blue, the other in red glass. The shapes in this series were influenced by Chinese porcelains, the finish inspired by Eastern lacquers.
Acid stamped: *venini murano MADE IN ITALY*; unsigned.
8.5" high (cm. 21)
8.75" high (cm. 22)

Exhibitions:
1940, Venice, 22nd Biennale Internazionale d'Arte.

Bibliography and comparative texts:
Venini blue catalogue, n. 3575;
G. Ponti, 1940, p. 71;
F. Deboni, 1989, n. 67;
M. Barovier, 1991, n. 37;
M. Barovier, R. Barovier Mentasti,
A. Dorigato, 1995, n. 56;
M. Barovier, 1997, p. 215;
M. Barovier, 1998b, p. 26;
M. Barovier, 1999, p. 187.

59. Carlo Scarpa
Venini & C.

Cinesi, 1940

Two vases in red glass. The shapes in this series were influenced by Chinese porcelains, the finish inspired by Eastern lacquers.
Acid stamped: *venini murano MADE IN ITALY* and *venini murano ITALIA*.
14" high (cm. 35.5)
10" high (cm. 25)

Exhibitions:
1940, Venice, 22nd Biennale Internazionale d'Arte.

Bibliography and comparative texts:
Venini blue catalogue, n. 3933;
G. Ponti, 1940, p. 71;
F. Deboni, 1989, n. 67;
M. Barovier, 1991, n. 37;
M. Barovier, R. Barovier Mentasti,
A. Dorigato, 1995, n. 56;
M. Barovier, 1997, p. 215;
M. Barovier, 1998b, p. 26;
M. Barovier, 1999, p. 187.

Cinesi vases; photo from the archives.

60. Carlo Scarpa
Venini & C.

Inciso, 1940

Cylindrical vase in transparent light blue glass cased in amethyst. The wheel-cut carvings are undulating vertical lines.
Identified with a paper label: *Venini n. 3753*.
11.5" high (cm. 29)

Exhibitions:
1940, Milan, 7th Triennale.

Bibliography and comparative texts:
Venini blue catalogue, nn. 3753;
R. Papini, 1940, p. 221;
G. Ponti, 1940, p. 58, 61;
Lo Stile, 1941, p. 60;
Domus, 1953, December, p. 70;
G. Ponti, 1959, p. 34;
Space Design, 1977, p. 69;
G. Duplani Tucci, 1989, n. 22;
M. Barovier, 1991, nn. 43, 44;
M. Barovier, R. Barovier Mentasti,
A. Dorigato, 1995, pp. 49, 52;
Gli Artisti..., 1996, nn. 104, 105, 106, 107;

M. Barovier, 1997, p. 218;
M. Barovier, 1998b, p. 28.

Venini display at the 7th Triennale, Milan, 1940.

61. Carlo Scarpa
Venini & C.

Velato e Inciso, 1940

A tall vase composed of
straw-colored glass. Decorated
with horizontal bands of *inciso*.
The entire surface is finished in
the *velato* technique.
Paper label: Venini
12.5" high (cm. 32)

Exhibitions:
1940, Milan, 7th Esposizione
Internazionale d'Arte.

Bibliography and comparative texts:
Venini blue catalogue, n. 3791;
G. Ponti, 1940, p. 72;
F. Deboni, 1989, n. 74;
M. Barovier, 1997, pp. 152, 281.

62. Carlo Scarpa
Venini & C.

Battuto, 1940

A transparent amethyst vase with the
surface finished with light horizontal
carvings.
14" high (cm. 35.5)

Exhibitions:
1940, Venice, 22nd Biennale
Internazionale d'Arte;
1940, Milan, 7th Triennale.

Bibliography and comparative texts:
Venini blue catalogue, n. 3940;
G. Ponti, 1940, p. 70;
R. Aloi, 1945, nn. 10, 13;
M. Brusatin, 1972, p. 24;
Carlo Scarpa..., 1984, p. 185;
La verrerie..., 1988, p. 117;
F. Deboni, 1989, n. 58-63;
M. Barovier, 1991, n. 23, 32;
R. Barovier Mentasti, 1992, n. 69;
M. Barovier, R. Barovier Mentasti,

A. Dorigato, 1995, n. 54;
F. Deboni, 1996, n. 193;
Gli Artisti..., 1996, nn. 98-104;
Italienisches..., 1996, nn. 42, 43;
M. Barovier, 1997, p. 219;
M. Barovier, 1998b, p. 27;
M. Barovier, 1999, p. 187.

63. Carlo Scarpa
Venini & C.

Velato, 1940

A bowl in thin light straw-colored
glass. The entire surface is finely
ground to a satin finish.
Acid stamped: *venini murano.*
4.5" high (cm. 11)
7.5" Ø (cm. 19)

Exhibitions:
1940, Venice, 22nd Biennale
Internazionale d'Arte;
1940, Milan, 7th Triennale.

Bibliography and comparative texts:
Venini blue catalogue, n. 3766;
G. Ponti, 1940, p. 71;
C.E. Rava, 1943, p. 131;
F. Deboni, 1989, p. 24;
M. Barovier, 1991, n. 33;
M. Barovier, 1997, p. 217;
M. Barovier, 1998b, p. 28.

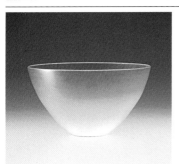

64. Carlo Scarpa
Venini & C.

Battuti, 1940

Three glass vases. One black,
one yellow and one *lattimo*.
All three vases are cased in
straw-colored glass with the entire
surface finished at the carving wheel.
Acid stamped: *venini murano ITALIA.*
16.25" high (cm. 41)
8" high (cm. 20)
14.5" high (cm. 37)

Exhibitions:
1940, Venice, 22nd Biennale
Internazionale d'Arte;
1940, Milan, 7th Triennale.

Bibliography and comparative texts:
Venini blue catalogue, nn. 3919,
3943 A, 3939; G. Ponti, 1940, p. 70;
R. Aloi, 1945, nn. 10, 13;
M. Brusatin, 1972, p. 24;
Carlo Scarpa..., 1984, p. 185;
La verrerie..., 1988, p. 117;
F. Deboni, 1989, n. 58-63;
M. Barovier, 1991, nn. 23, 32;
R. Barovier Mentasti, 1992, n. 69;
M. Barovier, R. Barovier Mentasti,

A. Dorigato, 1995, n. 54;
F. Deboni, 1996, n. 193;
Gli Artisti..., 1996, nn. 98-104;
Italienisches..., 1996, nn. 42,43;
M. Barovier, 1997, p. 219;
M. Barovier, 1998b, p. 27;
M. Barovier, 1999, p. 187.

Vases published in *Arredamento
Moderno* in 1945.

65. Carlo Scarpa
Venini & C.

Murrine opache, 1940

Red, black and yellow *murrine* bowl.
The bottom of the bowl is composed
of lemon yellow *murrine*, the sides of
red *murrine*. The entire surface is
finished at the carving wheel,
creating an opaque effect.
14.5" x 9" x 2.5" (cm. 36,5 x 23 x 6.5)

Exhibitions:
1940, Venice, 22nd Biennale
Internazionale d'Arte.

Bibliography and comparative texts:
Venini grey catalogue, n. 4871;
G. Dell'Oro, 1940, p. 54;
G. Ponti, 1940, p. 69;
Domus, 1951, October, p. 29;
G. Mariacher, 1954, p. 169;
R. Aloi, 1955, p. 22;
A. Gasparetto, 1960, n. 37;
Mille anni..., 1982, n. 531;
R. Barovier Mentasti, 1982, p. 283;
W. Neuwirth, 1987, p. 200;
F. Deboni, 1989, nn. 65, 71, 72, 73;

G. Duplani Tucci, 1989, nn. 15, 21;
H. Ricke, 1990, p. 23;
M. Barovier, 1991, nn. 45, 51;
Vetri di Murano..., 1991, p. 119;
L'arte del vetro..., 1992, p. 251;
M. Barovier, 1994, nn. 9, 11;
M. Barovier, R. Barovier Mentasti,
A. Dorigato, 1995, n. 59;
F. Deboni, 1996, n. 197;
Gli Artisti..., 1996, n. 113;
Italienisches..., 1996, nn. 37, 38;
M. Barovier, 1997, p. 221;
Il vetro italiano..., 1998, n. 97;
M. Barovier, 1999, p. 187.

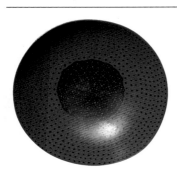

66. Carlo Scarpa
Venini & C.

Murrine opache, 1940

A bowl composed of *pasta vitrea* black and red *murrine*. The entire surface is finished at the carving wheel, creating an opaque effect.
Paper label: *Venini n. 4883*.
11" Ø (cm. 28)
3" high (cm. 7)

Exhibition:
1940, Venice, 22nd Biennale Internazionale d'Arte.

Bibliography and comparative texts:
Venini grey catalogue, n. 4871;
G. Dell'Oro, 1940, p. 54;
G. Ponti, 1940, p. 69;
Domus, 1951, October, p. 29;
G. Mariacher, 1954, p. 169;
R. Aloi, 1955, p. 22;
A. Gasparetto, 1960, n. 37
Mille anni..., 1982, n. 531
R. Barovier Mentasti, 1982, p. 283;
W. Neuwirth, 1987, p. 200;
F. Deboni, 1989, nn. 65, 71, 72, 73;

G. Duplani Tucci, 1989, nn. 15, 21;
H. Ricke, 1990, p. 23;
M. Barovier, 1991, nn. 45, 51;
Vetri di Murano..., 1991, p. 119;
L'arte del vetro..., 1992, p. 251;
M. Barovier, 1994, nn. 9, 11;
M. Barovier, R. Barovier Mentasti, A. Dorigato, 1995, n. 59;
F. Deboni, 1996, n. 197;
Gli Artisti..., 1996, n. 113;
Italienisches..., 1996, nn. 37, 38;
M. Barovier, 1997, p. 221;
Il vetro italiano..., 1998, n. 97;
M. Barovier, 1999, p. 187.

67. Carlo Scarpa
Venini & C.

A murrine, 1940 ca.
Piatto del Serpente, 1940

A canoe-shaped *a murrine* bowl. The *murrine* are red and black, black and red, and yellow and black. The entire surface is finished at the carving wheel.
Paper label: *Venini n. 4883*.
13" (cm. 31)

A black *pasta vitrea* murrine bowl, decorated with white and red *murrine* arranged to look like a serpent twisted into a spiral.
Engraved: *venini italia*.
14.5" x 9.75" x 2.5"
(cm. 37 x 25 x 6.5)

Exhibitions:
1940, Venice, 22nd Biennale Internazionale d'Arte.

Bibliography and comparative texts:
Venini grey catalogue, n. 4873;
G. Dell'Oro, 1940, p. 54;
G. Ponti, 1940, p. 69;

Domus, 1951, October, p. 29;
G. Mariacher, 1954, p. 169;
R. Aloi, 1955, p. 22;
A. Gasparetto, 1960, n. 37;
Mille anni..., 1982, n. 531;
R. Barovier Mentasti, 1982, p. 283;
W. Neuwirth, 1987, p. 200;
F. Deboni, 1989, nn. 65, 71, 72, 73;
G. Duplani Tucci, 1989, nn. 15, 21;
The Venetians..., 1989, n. 32;
H. Ricke, 1990, p. 23;
M. Barovier, 1991, nn. 45, 51;
Vetri di Murano..., 1991, p. 119;
L'arte del vetro..., 1992, p. 251;
M. Barovier, 1994, nn. 9, 11;
M. Barovier, R. Barovier Mentasti,

A. Dorigato, 1995, n. 59;
F. Deboni, 1996, n. 197;
Gli Artisti..., 1996, n. 113;
Italienisches..., 1996, nn. 37, 38;
M. Barovier, 1997, p. 221;
Il vetro italiano..., 1998, n. 97;
M. Barovier, 1999, p. 187.

68. Carlo Scarpa
Venini & C.

A fasce, 1942

A double gourd-shaped vase composed of lightly iridized clear glass decorated with horizontal *fasce* of colored glass.
Acid stamped (circular):
venini murano.
8.25" high (cm. 21)

Exhibitions:
1942, Venice, 23rd Biennale Internazionale d'Arte.

Bibliography and comparative texts:
Venini grey catalogue, n. 4562;
G. Ponti, 1959, p. 42;
Vetri di Murano..., 1981, p. 105;
W. Neuwirth, 1987, p. 216;
F. Deboni, 1989, nn. 80, 81, 85;
G. Duplani Tucci, 1989, n. 19;
The Venetians..., n. 13;
M. Barovier, 1991, n. 56;
M. Barovier, R. Barovier Mentasti, A. Dorigato, 1995, nn. 70, 73;
F. Deboni, 1996, nn. 200, 201;

Gli Artisti..., 1996, n. 120;
M. Heiremans, 1996, n. 69;
Italienisches..., 1996, n. 44;
M. Barovier, 1997, p. 222;
M. Barovier, 1998b, p. 31;
M. Barovier, 1999, p. 186.

---

69. Carlo Scarpa
Venini & C.

A fili, 1942

A clear glass vase decorated with horizontal *fili* (threads) of colored glass. The entire surface is lightly *battuto* (etched) horizontally.
7.25" high (cm. 18)

Exhibitions:
1942, Venice, 23rd Biennale Internazionale d'Arte.

Bibliography and comparative texts:
G. Ponti, 1959, p. 42;
Vetri Murano..., 1981, p. 105;
W. Neuwirth, 1987, p. 216;
F. Deboni, 1989, nn. 80, 81, 85;
G. Duplani Tucci, 1989, n. 19;
The Venetians..., n. 13;
M. Barovier, 1991, n. 56;
M. Barovier, R. Barovier Mentasti, A. Dorigato, 1995, nn. 70, 73;
F. Deboni, 1996, nn. 200, 201;
Gli Artisti..., 1996, n. 120;

M. Heiremans, 1996, n. 69;
Italienisches..., 1996, n. 44;
M. Barovier, 1997, p. 222;
M. Barovier, 1998b, n. 31;
M. Barovier, 1999, p. 186.

70. Carlo Scarpa
Venini & C.

A fasce applicate, 1940

A clear glass shallow bowl with a strongly iridized surface, decorated with aqua and red *fasce* applicate.
10" x 8.75" (cm. 25 x 22)

Exhibitions:
1940, Milan, 7th Triennale.

Bibliography and comparative texts:
Venini grey catalogue, n. 4476;
G. Ponti, 1940, p. 61;
F. Deboni, 1989, n. 66;
M. Barovier, 1991, n. 61;
M. Heiremans, 1996, n. 62;
Italienisches..., 1996, n. 28;
M. Barovier, 1997, p. 220;
M. Barovier, 1998b, p. 28.

71. Carlo Scarpa
Venini & C.

A fasce, 1942

A glass vase. The top portion is
composed of clear glass, iridized to
appear pale dusty rose, the bottom
portion is aquamarine. The two parts
are separated by an aubergine
fascia of glass.
Acid stamped: *Venini murano.*
10" high (cm. 25)

Bibliography and comparative texts:
G. Ponti, 1959, p. 42;
Vetri Murano..., 1981, p. 105;
W. Neuwirth, 1987, p. 216;
F. Deboni, 1989, nn. 80, 81, 85;
G. Duplani Tucci, 1989, n. 19;
The Venetians..., n. 13;
M. Barovier, 1991, n. 56;
M. Barovier, R. Barovier Mentasti,
A. Dorigato, 1995, nn. 70, 73;
F. Deboni, 1996, nn. 200, 201;
Gli Artisti..., 1996, n. 120;
M. Heiremans, 1996, n. 69;
Italienisches..., 1996, n. 44;
M. Barovier, 1997, p. 222;
M. Barovier, 1998b, n. 31;

M. Barovier, 1999, p. 186.

Venini glass pieces at an exhibition;
photo from the archives.

72. Carlo Scarpa
Venini & C.

A pennellate, 1942

Vase in lightly iridized clear glass,
decorated with *a pennellate*
(brushstrokes) of yellow and
amethyst glass.
10.5" high (cm. 26)

Exhibitions:
1942, Venice, 23rd Biennale
Internazionale d'Arte.

Bibliography and comparative texts:
Catalogue, n. 4541;
G. Ponti, 1959, p. 42;
Space Design, 1977, p. 70;
Vetro di Murano..., 1982, n. 146;
Venini & the Murano..., 1984, n. 12;
W. Neuwirth, 1987, p. 216;
F. Deboni, 1989, n. 82;
R. Barovier Mentasti, 1992, n. 65;
H. Newman, 1993, p. 298;
M. Barovier, R. Barovier Mentasti,
A. Dorigato, 1995, n. 72;

Glas Band II, 1995, p. 229;
Venezia e la Biennale..., 1995, p. 430;
F. Deboni, 1996, n. 199;
Gli Artisti, 1996, nn. 121, 122;
M. Heiremans, 1996, n. 68;
Italienisches..., 1996, n. 45;
M. Barovier, 1997, p. 223;
M. Barovier, 1998b, p. 30;
Venini Venezia, 1998, p. 67;
M. Barovier, 1999, p. 187.

73. Carlo Scarpa
Venini & C.

A pennellate, 1942

Bowl in lightly iridized clear glass,
decorated with *a pennellate*
(brushstrokes) of yellow and
amethyst glass.
Acid stamped: *venini murano ITALIA.*
4.5" high (cm. 11.5);
8.5" Ø (cm. 21.5)

Exhibitions:
1942, Venice, 23rd Biennale
Internazionale d'Arte.

Bibliography and comparative texts:
Venini blue catalogue n. 3779.
In addition, see description n. 72.

Venini display at the 23rd Biennale
Internazionale d'Arte, Venice, 1942.

74. Carlo Scarpa
Venini & C.

A pennellate, 1942

Two vases and a bowl in lightly
iridized clear glass, decorated with *a
pennellate* (brushstrokes). The vase
on the left is in shades of aubergines.
The tall vase is in shades of blue
and the bowl is in shades of pink.
Unsigned; Acid stamped: *venini
murano* and *venini murano ITALIA.*
5.25" high (cm. 13)
9.5" high (cm. 24)
5.25" high (cm. 13) 7.75" Ø (cm. 20)

Exhibitions:
1942, Venice, 23rd Biennale
Internazionale d'Arte

Bibliography and comparative texts:
Venini blue catalogue nn. 3911, 3767.
In addition, see description n. 72.

A pennellate vessels; photo from the
archives.

75. Carlo Scarpa
Venini & C.

Decoro a fili, 1942

Bowl in clear glass decorated with
shades of brown *fili* (threads).
The entire surface is highly iridized.
Acid stamped: *venini murano ITALIA.*
3.5" high (cm. 9)
10" Ø (cm. 25)

Bibliography and comparative texts:
Venini grey catalogue, n. 4569;
M. Barovier, 1991, n. 53;
Italienisches..., 1996, n. 48;
M. Barovier, 1997, p. 224.

76. Carlo Scarpa
Venini & C.

Conchiglie, 1942

Three seashells. The shell on the top is composed of clear *cristallo*, the middle is straw-colored and the bottom pink. All three are strongly iridized.
All acid stamped: *venini murano MADE IN ITALY*, paper label; *venini murano ITALIA*; *venini murano MADE IN ITALY*.
6" Ø (cm. 15); 9" Ø (cm. 23); 7" Ø (cm. 18)

Exhibitions:
1942, Venice, 23rd Biennale Internazionale d'Arte.

Bibliography and comparative texts:
Venini grey catalogue, n. 4556;
R. Aloi, 1945, n. 23;
F. Deboni, 1989, nn. 77, 79;
M. Barovier, 1991, n. 57;
M. Barovier, R. Barovier Mentasti, A. Dorigato, 1995, p. 52;
Italienisches..., 1996, n. 49;
M. Barovier, 1997, p. 224.

77. Giò Ponti
Venini & C.

Bottiglie morandiane, 1946-1950

Three stoppered bottles from the Morandiane series composed of multicolored vertical glass canes. The canes on the stoppers match the canes on the bottles.
Acid stamped: *venini murano ITALIA*.
16" high (cm. 40)
14" high (cm. 36)
18" high (cm. 47)

Bibliography and comparative texts:
Venini green catalogue, nn. 526.10, 526.12, 526.08; G. Ponti, 1959, p. 41;
A. Gasparetto, 1960, n. 43;
W. Neuwirth, 1987, n. 39, pp. 218, 220;
G. Duplani Tucci, 1989, pp. 54, 55, n. 27;
F. Deboni, 1989, n. 88;
M. Heiremans, 1993, n. 207;
M. Heiremans, 1996, n. 165;
Italienisches..., 1996, n. 110;
Venini Venezia, 1998, p. 68.

78. Giò Ponti
Venini & C.

Bottiglie morandiane, 1946-1950

Two *incalmo* bottles. One has the base and stopper in *lattimo*, the other base and stopper are blue *pasta vitrea*. Both have the neck in transparent grey glass.
Acid stamped: *venini murano ITALIA*.
13.75" high (cm. 35)
13.75" high (cm. 35)

Bibliography and comparative texts:
Venini grey catalogue, nn. 4491;
Domus, 1950, November/December;
G. Ponti, 1959, p. 41;
A. Gasparetto, 1960, n. 43;
W. Neuwirth, 1987, n. 39, pp. 218, 220;
G. Duplani Tucci, 1989, pp. 54, 55, n. 27;
F. Deboni, 1989, n. 88;
M. Heiremans, 1993, n. 207;
M. Heiremans, 1996, n. 165;
Italienisches..., 1996, n. 110;
Venini Venezia, 1998, p. 68.

79. Giò Ponti
Venini & C.

Bottiglie morandiane, 1946-1950

Two stoppered *incalmo* bottles from the *Morandiane* series. One is straw and light aubergine glass with a straw colored stopper, the other is straw and blue glass with a blue stopper.
Acid stamped: *venini murano ITALIA*.
13.5" high (cm. 34)
13.5" high (cm. 34)

Bibliography and comparative texts:
Venini grey catalogue, nn. 4492;
G. Ponti, 1959, p. 41;
A. Gasparetto, 1960, n. 43;
W. Neuwirth, 1987, n. 39, pp. 218, 220;
G. Duplani Tucci, 1989, pp. 54, 55, n. 27;
F. Deboni, 1989, n. 88;
M. Heiremans, 1993, n. 207;
M. Heiremans, 1996, n. 165;
Italienisches..., 1996, n. 110;
Venini Venezia, 1998, p. 68.

Bottiglie morandiane published in the December, 1959 issue of *Domus*.

80. Fulvio Bianconi and Paolo Venini
Venini & C.

Fazzoletti, 1948 ca.

Three *fazzoletti* (handkerchiefs) vases. The one on the left is composed of *lattimo* glass *incamiciato* in red glass; the one in the center is turquoise opaline glass; the one on the right is iridescent green glass.
Acid stamped: *venini murano MADE IN ITALY*, *venini murano* (circular signature), and *venini murano ITALIA*.

4.5" high (cm. 11)
3" high (cm. 8)
5" high (cm. 12)

Bibliography and comparative texts:
Venini grey catalogue, nn. 2987, 1157, 4241;
Domus, November/December, 1950;
R. Aloi, 1952, n. 10;
A. Gasparetto, 1960, n. 36;
B. Nerozzi, 1987, n. 120;
W. Neuwirth, 1987, n. 53;
F. Deboni, 1989, n. 106;
The Venetians..., 1989, n. 28;
R. Bossaglia, 1993, n. 21;
Italienisches..., 1996, n. 67.

81. Fulvio Bianconi and Paolo Venini
Venini & C.

Fazzoletti, 1948-1950

Two *fazzoletti* (handkerchiefs) vases. One composed of *lattimo* glass *incamiciato* in black glass; the other is in *lattimo* glass *incamiciato* in red glass with a slightly iridized surface. Acid stamped: *venini murano ITALIA*.
10" high (cm. 25.5)
10" high (cm. 25.5)

Bibliography and comparative texts:
Domus, November/December, 1950;
R. Aloi, 1952, n. 10;
A. Gasparetto, 1960, n. 36;
B. Nerozzi, 1987, n. 120;
W. Neuwirth, 1987, n. 53;
F. Deboni, 1989, n. 106;
The Venetians..., 1989, n. 28;
R. Bossaglia, 1993, n. 21;
Italienisches..., 1996, n. 67.

82. Fulvio Bianconi and Paolo Venini
Venini & C.

Fazzoletti, 1950 ca.

Three *fazzoletti* (handkerchiefs) vases. The one on the left is clear glass decorated with canes of *filigrana* and *zanfirico lattimo*; the one in the center has amethyst and *lattimo* canes of *filigrana*, the one on the right is *zanfirico lattimo*. Acid stamped: *venini murano ITALIA*.

7" high (cm. 17)
4" high (cm. 10)
11" high (cm. 28)

Exhibitions:
1952, Venice, 26th Biennale Internazionale d'Arte.

Bibliography and comparative texts:
Venini grey catalogue, nn. 4217, 1158, 2986; *Domus*, October, 1951, p. 29;
R. Aloi, 1952, n. 29;
G. Ponti, 1959, p. 38;
Mille anni..., 1982, n. 649;
R. Barovier Mentasti, 1982, n. 323;
W. Neuwirth, 1987, n. 75;
R. Bossaglia, 1993, nn. 17, 20;
M. Barovier, 1994, nn. 14, 15;
F. Deboni, 1996, nn. 206, 207;
Gli Artisti..., 1996, nn. 130, 132;
M. Heiremans, 1996, n. 84;
Italienisches..., 1996, n. 69;
M. Barovier, 1998b, p. 231;
Venini Venezia, 1998, p. 68;
M. Barovier, 1999, p. 231.

83. Fulvio Bianconi
Venini & C.

A macchie, 1950

Vase composed of *cristallo* glass decorated with an abstract pattern obtained by the inclusion of aubergine *macchie* (stains) of glass. Acid stamped: *venini murano ITALIA*.
10" high (cm. 25)

Exhibitions:
1950, Venice, 25th Biennale Internazionale d'Arte;
1951, Milano, 9th Triennale;
1952, Venice, 26th Biennale Internazionale d'Arte.

Bibliography and comparative texts:
Venini grey catalogue, n. 4324;
A. Gasparetto, 1960, n. 37;
F. Deboni, 1989, n. 116;
G. Duplani Tucci, 1989, n. 36;
M. Heiremans, 1993, n. 218;
R. Bossaglia, 1993, n. 34;
M. Barovier, R. Barovier Mentasti, A. Dorigato, 1995, n. 83;
F. Deboni, 1996, p. 74, n. 212;
M. Heiremans, 1996, n. 89;
Italienisches..., 1996, nn. 73, 74;
Venini Venezia, 1998, p. 71;
M. Barovier, 1999, p. 227.

A macchie vases published in the October 1950 issue of *Domus*.

84. Fulvio Bianconi
Venini & C.

A spicchi, 1950

A flask shaped vase composed of *cristallo* glass; one side decorated with six *spicchi*; triangular segments of aubergine, straw and blue colored glass.
10" high (cm. 25)

Bibliography and comparative texts:
Venini grey catalogue, n. 4316;
Domus, October, 1950;
Domus, August, 1952;
G. Mariacher, 1967, p. 172;
F. Deboni, 1989, n. 109;
M. Heiremans, 1989, n. 200;
R. Bossaglia, 1993, n. 36;
M. Heiremans, 1993, n. 221;
Italienisches..., 1996, n. 86;
Gli Artisti..., 1996, n. 152;
Venini Venezia, 1998, p. 70.

Venini vases published in the October, 1950 issue of *Domus*.

85. Fulvio Bianconi
Venini & C.

Pezzato, 1951

A *pezzato* (patchwork) vase. The patches are in transparent glass and *pasta vitrea* in red, white, green and shades of blue. Acid stamped: *venini murano ITALIA*.
15" high (cm. 38)

Bibliography and comparative texts:
Venini grey catalogue, n. 4319;
R. Aloi, 1952, n. 29;
R. Aloi, 1955, p. 20;
L'arte del vetro, 1992, n. 358;
R. Bossaglia, 1993, nn. 53, 54;
M. Barovier, 1994, n. 21;
F. Deboni, 1996, n. 215;
Italienisches..., 1996, n. 83;
Venini Venezia, 1998, p. 71;
H. Lockwood, 1995, p. 8.

Two *pezzati* and a *scozzese* vases published in *Vetri d'oggi*, 1955.

86. Fulvio Bianconi
Venini & C.

Pezzato, 1950-1951

A *pezzato* (patchwork) vase.
Composed of transparent patches in
black, turquoise, clear, and straw.
Acid stamped: *venini murano ITALIA*.
9.5" high (cm. 24)

Exhibitions:
1951, Milan, 9th Triennale;
1952, Venice, 26th Biennale
Internazionale d'Arte.

Bibliography and comparative texts:
Venini grey catalogue, n. 1329.

87. Fulvio Bianconi
Venini & C.

Pezzati, 1951-1952 ca.

Three *pezzati* (patchwork) vases.
The one on the left is in the *Istanbul*
colors, composed of transparent
patches in clear, straw, and tan.
The middle vase is in the *Parigi*
colors composed of transparent
patches in blue, green, clear and
red. The vase on the right is in the
Stoccolma colors, composed of
transparent patches in black,
turquoise, clear, and straw.

Acid stamped: *venini murano ITALIA*.
Paper label *n. 4916*
8.25" high (cm. 21)
9" high (cm. 23)
9" high (cm. 23)

Exhibitions:
1951, Milan, 9th Triennale;
1952, Venice, 26th Biennale
Internazionale d'Arte.

Bibliography and comparative texts:
Venini grey catalogue, n. 4916, 1329;
R. Aloi, 1955, p. 20;
G. Ponti, 1959, p. 42;
W. Neuwirth, 1987, n. 35;

F. Deboni, 1989, n. 107;
R. Bossaglia, 1993, n. 68;
M. Barovier, 1994, n. 20;
M. Barovier, R. Barovier Mentasti,
A. Dorigato, 1995, n. 104;
F. Deboni, 1996, n. 214;
Italienisches..., 1996, nn. 77, 78, 79, 80;
Gli Artisti..., 1996, nn. 145, 146, 147;
H. Lockwood, 1995, p. 8.

88. Fulvio Bianconi
Venini & C.

Sirena, 1950

Torso-shaped vessel in transparent
green glass decorated with a
webbing of applied *lattimo* glass.
Acid stamped: *venini murano ITALIA*.
Paper label: *Venini Murano MADE
IN ITALY*.
16" high (cm. 40).

Bibliography and comparative texts:
Venini grey catalogue, n. 4209;
The Venetians..., 1989, n. 24;
R. Bossaglia, 1993, n. 43;
M. Heiremans, 1993, n. 223;
F. Deboni, 1996, n. 210;
M. Heiremans, 1996, n. 90;
Italienisches..., 1996, n. 85;
H. Lockwood, 1998, p. 19.

89. Fulvio Bianconi
Venini & C.

A fasce orizzontali 1951

Vase in transparent straw-colored
glass decorated with orange *fasce*.
Acid stamped: *venini murano ITALIA*.
Paper label.
9" high (cm. 23)

Bibliography and comparison texts:
Venini grey catalogue, n. 4400;
The Venetians..., 1989, n. 17.

90. Fulvio Bianconi
Venini & C.

A fasce orizzontali, 1953

Vase in *cristallo* with horizontal *fasce*
in aubergine, red, green and blue
glass.
Acid stamped: *venini murano ITALIA*.
19.5" high (cm. 49.5)

Bibliography and comparative texts:
Domus, 1956, January;
A. Gasparetto, 1958, n. 190;
F. Deboni, 1989, n. 117;
R. Bossaglia, 1993, nn. 65, 66;
M. Heiremans, 1993, n. 235;
Gli Artisti..., 1996, n. 156;
Italienisches..., 1996, n. 91.

Vessels in a *fasce orizzontali*
published in *Domus*, January 1956
issue.

91. Fulvio Bianconi
Venini & C.

A canne, 1951

A tall bottle made with thin green and blue glass canes, composed of two flattened orbs, one resting on top of the other at a 90° angle. A matching flattened orb stopper.
Acid stamped: *venini murano ITALIA*.
22.5" high (cm. 56.5)

Exhibitions:
1951, Milan, 9th Triennale.

Bibliography and comparative texts:
Venini grey catalogue, n. 4404;
G. Ponti, 1959;
W. Neuwirth, 1987, n. 186;
M. Heiremans, 1993, n. 215;
Italienisches..., 1996, n. 76.

Venini bottles published in the April, 1962 issue of *Domus*.

92. Fulvio Bianconi
Venini & C.

A fasce e a canne, 1951-1956

Four bottles. Two, (first and third) with horizontal *fasce*: the first in yellow transparent glass with an opaque aubergine *fascia*, the third in transparent grey with a yellow opaque *fascia*. The other two (second and fourth) are made with vertical canes: the second in transparent blue and green canes, the fourth in opaque yellow and transparent blue canes with a matching stopper.

Acid stamped: *venini murano ITALIA*.
12" high (cm. 30)
15" high (cm. 38)
12" high (cm. 30)
18" high (cm. 45)

Bibliography and comparative texts:
Venini grey catalogue, n. 4479;
Venini green catalogue, n. 526.10.
In addition, see description n. 91.

93. Fulvio Bianconi
Venini & C.

A fasce, 1950

Bottle-shaped vase in transparent turquoise green glass, decorated with two applied wide opaque *fasce* of glass, one red and one orange; the neck is covered with a layer of aubergine glass.
Acid stamped: *venini murano ITALIA*.
14" high (cm. 35)

Exhibitions:
1950, Venice, 25th Biennale Internazionale d'Arte;
1951, Milan, 9th Triennale;
1952, Venice, 26th Biennale Internazionale d'Arte.

Bibliography and comparative texts:
Venini grey catalogue, n. 4315;
photo n. 512, A.S.A.C., Venice;
R. Aloi, 1955, p. 13;
G. Ponti, 1959;
La Verrerie..., 1988, n. 2;
F. Deboni, 1989, n. 125;
The Venetians..., 1989, n. 20;
R. Bossaglia, 1993, n. 67;

M. Heiremans, 1993, n. 221;
M. Barovier, R. Barovier Mentasti, A. Dorigato, 1995, p. 64;
M. Heiremans, 1996, n. 95;
Italienisches..., 1996, n. 81;
Il vetro italiano..., 1998, n. 130.

Vessels in *a fasce* glass published in the December, 1959 issue of *Domus*.

94. Fulvio Bianconi
Venini & C.

A fasce orizzontali, 1951-1956

Two stoppered bottles, one in transparent blue and one in grey glass, both decorated with two applied wide opaque *fasce* of red glass. Matching stoppers with applied
red *fasce*.
Acid stamped: *venini murano ITALIA*.
16" high (cm. 40)
15" high (cm. 38)

Exhibitions:
1956, Venice, 28th Biennale Internazionale d'Arte.

Bibliography and comparative texts:
Venini grey catalogue, n. 4582;
G. Ponti, 1959;
A. Gasparetto, 1960, n. 36;
W. Neuwirth, 1987, n. 34, p. 186;
F. Deboni, 1989, n. 122;
M. Heiremans, 1996, n. 166;
Designed for Delight, 1997, n. 75.

Bottles in *a fasce* glass published in the December, 1959 issue of *Domus*.

95. Fulvio Bianconi
Venini & C.

Sasso, 1965

Vessel designed to appear like a *sasso* (rock). Composed of two parts in coral red *pasta vitrea* separated by a band of transparent light blue glass. The finish of the blue glass is lightly *battuto*. This vessel is shaped while hot and is not blown.
Engraved: *venini ITALIA*.
4.5" high (cm. 11,5)

Bibliography and comparative texts:
F. Deboni, 1989, nn. 167, 168;
The Venetians..., 1989, n. 52;
R. Bossaglia, 1993, nn. 98, 99;
M. Heiremans, 1993, n. 246;
F. Deboni, 1996, n. 230;
M. Heiremans, 1996, nn. 236, 237;
Italienisches..., 1996, nn. 106, 107;
Venini Venezia, 1998, p. 76;
M. Barovier, 1999, p. 267;

96. Fulvio Bianconi
Venini & C.

Informale, 1968

A sculptural vase in transparent aquamarine glass with a rough surface.
Engraved: *venini ITALIA*.
18" high (cm. 45)

Bibliography and comparative texts:
Venini green catalogue, n. 711;
M. Heiremans, 1989, n. 222;
R. Bossaglia, 1993, n. 100;
M. Heiremans, 1993, n. 247;
Gli Artisti..., 1996, n. 235;
Italienisches..., 1996, n. 108;
Venini Venezia, 1998, p. 79.

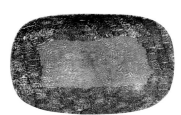

97. Paolo Venini
Venini & C.

A murrine, 1959

Grey and *lattimo murrine* bowl.
The bottom of the bowl is composed of turquoise and *lattimo murrine*.
Paper label: Venini 4880.
8.75" x 5.25" high (cm. 22 x 14)

Bibliography and comparative texts:
Venini grey catalogue, n. 4880;
G. Ponti, 1959;
F. Deboni, 1989, n. 153;
The Venetians..., 1989, n. 33;
Gli Artisti..., 1996, n. 180;
Italienisches..., 1996, n. 148.

98. Paolo Venini
Venini & C.

Mosaico Zanfirico, 1954

Transparent blue glass vase decorated with horizontal and vertical segments of *zanfirico lattimo* canes.
Acid stamped: *venini murano ITALIA*.
13.5" high (cm. 34)

Exhibitions:
1954, Milan, 10th Triennale;
1954, Venice, 27th Biennale Internazionale d'Arte.

Bibliography and comparative texts:
Venini grey catalogue, n. 3886;
G. Ponti, 1959;
Domus, 1955, April;
W. Neuwirth, 1987, n. 69;
F. Deboni, 1989, nn. 126, 127, 128;
The Venetians..., 1989, n. 34;
M. Barovier, 1994, n. 17;
F. Deboni, 1996, p. 74, n. 221;
M. Heiremans, 1996, n. 152;
Italienisches..., 1996, nn. 116, 117, 118;

Il vetro italiano...,1998, n.129;
M. Barovier, 1999, p. 231;

Vases in *mosaico zanfirico* published in the April, 1955 issue of *Domus*.

99. Paolo Venini
Venini & C.

Clessidre, 1955 ca.

Group of eight transparent glass *incalmo clessidre* (hourglasses) in various color combinations.
Acid stamped: *venini murano ITALIA*.
5.5" to 12" high (cm. 14 to 30)

Bibliography and comparative texts:
Venini grey catalogue, nn. 4905, 4906, 4907;
A. Gasparetto, 1960, n. 42
G. Mariacher, 1967, p. 169
F. Deboni, 1989, n. 132
G. Duplano Tucci, 1989, nn. 5, 6.

Clessidre in transparent glass; photo from the archives.

100. B.B.P.R.
Venini & C.

A fasce, 1954

Ceiling lamp in translucent glass decorated with irregular horizontal *fasce* in red, aubergine, blue and green glass. This model was designed by Studio Architetti B.B.P.R. for the New York City showroom of Olivetti.
Acid stamped: *venini murano ITALIA*.
26" high (cm. 66)

Bibliography and comparative texts:
Domus, 1954, September, pp. 3-9;
Domus, 1956, January, pp. 45, 46, 47, 48; G. Ponti, 1959.

Interior of Olivetti showroom in New York, *Domus*, December, 1959 issue.

101. Massimo Vignelli
Venini & C.

Sigaro, 1954

A cigar shaped ceiling lamp, the top portion composed of *lattimo* glass, the bottom a multicolored horizontal *fasce*.
Acid stamped: *venini murano ITALIA*.
14" high (cm. 35,5)

Bibliography and comparative texts:
Venini grey catalogue, n. 3035L;
Domus, 1956, November, p. 37;
G. Ponti, 1959;
Domus, 1956, January, pp. 45, 46, 47;
W. Neuwirth, 1987, n. 216;
Gli Artisti..., 1996, n. 163.

Lamps in *a fasce* glass published in the December, 1959 issue of *Domus*.

102. Massimo Vignelli
Venini & C.

Fungo, 1955

Table lamp composed of *lattimo* and yellow glass canes in the shape of a mushroom. Massimo Vignelli received an honorable mention at the Compasso d'Oro in 1956 for this design.
14" high (cm. 35,5)

Bibliography and comparative texts:
Stile Industria, 1956, December, n. 9;
Design Vignelli, 1990, p. 262;
Designed for Delight, 1997, n. 133;
Il vetro italiano..., 1998, n. 156.

103. Massimo Vignelli
Venini & C.

A fasce verticali, 1952

A pitcher and four drinking glasses, composed of transparent *fasce verticali* in pale colors.
Acid stamped: *venini murano*.
5" high (cm. 13)
12.5" high (cm. 32)

Bibliography and comparative texts:
Venini green catalogue, nn. 33c, 333.2; F. Deboni, 1989, n. 113;
Gli Artisti..., 1996, n. 162.

104. Massimo Vignelli
Venini & C.

Vetro e argento, 1957

Two transparent glass pitchers, one in aubergine and one in green, finished with dense wheel-carved cuts. Both fitted with silver handle and spout. The series was originally designed in 1957 for the American silversmith Towle but never produced. They were then produced by Venini and the French silversmith Christofle in 1960.
12" high (cm. 30); 10" high (cm. 25.5)

Bibliography and comparative texts:
Domus, 1963, July, pp. 39, 40;
Design Vignelli, 1990, p. 269;
Gli Artisti..., 1996, n. 214.

Vetro e argento vessels published in the July 1963 issue of *Domus*.

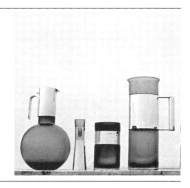

105. Massimo Vignelli
Venini & C.

Bicchieri e Brocca Ciga, 1979

Line of glassware designed by Massimo Vignelli and produced by Venini for the Ciga Hotels. The corrugation of the glass surface creates shadows and reflections and was designed to add brilliance and elegance to the glass.
7.25" high (cm. 18)
3.5" high (cm. 9)

Bibliography and comparative texts:
Design Vignelli, 1990, p. 272.

106. Giorgio Ferro
A.V.E.M. (Arte Vetraria Muranese)

Ansa volante, 1952

A vase with large handle in red translucent and iridescent glass.
10.75" high (cm. 17)

Exhibitions:
1952, Venice, 26th Biennale Internazionale d'Arte.

Bibliography and comparative texts:
B. Nerozzi, 1987, n. 53;
W. Neuwirth, 1987, n. 231;
M. Heiremans, 1989, nn. 3, 4, 5;
L'arte del vetro..., 1992, n. 376;
R. Barovier Mentasti, 1992, n. 95;
M. Barovier, R. Barovier Mentasti, A. Dorigato, 1995, n. 90;
Venezia e la Biennale..., 1995, n. 469;
F. Deboni, 1996, p. 23;
Italienisches..., 1996, n. 172;
M. Barovier, 1999, p. 191;

A.V.E.M. display at the 26th Biennale Internazionale d'Arte, Venice, 1952.

107. Giulio Radi
A.V.E.M. (Arte Vetraria Muranese)

Reazioni policrome, 1952

A *reazioni policrome* plate in aubergine glass with applications of gold leaf. The multicolored effects are due to the specific reactions of the added metallic oxides.
9" Ø (cm. 23)

Exhibitions:
1952, Venice, 26th Biennale Internazionale d'Arte.

Bibliography and comparative texts:
Venezianisches..., 1981, n. 127;
Mille anni..., 1982, n. 570;
R. Barovier Mentasti, 1982, n. 296;
Vetro di Murano, 1982, nn. 147, 148;
W. Neuwirth, 1987, p. 194;
M. Heiremans, 1989, n. 9;
M. Barovier, R. Barovier Mentasti, A. Dorigato, 1995, n. 89;
M. Barovier, 1999, p. 190.

108. Dino Martens
Aureliano Toso

Eldorado, 1952-1954

A vase with a central aperture from the *Eldorado* series. Composed of multicolored ground glass and *avventurina* with inclusions of *zanfirico* and *reticello* canes. This model corresponds to n. 5252 in the Aureliano Toso catalogue.
12" high (cm. 30)

Exhibitions:
1952, Venice, 26th Biennale Internazionale d'Arte.

Bibliography and comparative texts:
R. Aloi, 1955, p. 30;
M. Heiremans, 1993, nn. 163, 164;
M. Barovier, 1994, n. 25;
M. Heiremans, 1996, nn. 144, 145;
Italienisches..., 1996, n. 210;
L.M. Barbero, 1997, p. 231;
M. Barovier, 1999, p. 215.

109. Dino Martens
Aureliano Toso

Zanfirico, 1952

Vase from the *zanfirico* series. The clear glass is decorated with multicolored canes of *zanfirico* and *reticello* glass.
Paper Label: *Anita Kott importer*.
14.25" high (cm. 36)

Exhibitions:
1952, Venice, 26th Biennale Internazionale d'Arte.

Bibliography and comparative texts:
R. Aloi, 1952, n. 20;
R. Aloi, 1955, p. 31;
M. Heiremans, 1989, nn. 146, 147;
M. Heiremans, 1993, nn. 156, 166;
M. Barovier, 1994, n. 26;
M. Barovier, R. Barovier Mentasti, A. Dorigato, 1995, n. 97;
F. Deboni, 1996, p. 63, n. 150;
M. Heiremans, 1996, n. 103.

Vessels from the *Zanfirico* series; photo from the archives.

110. - 111. Dino Martens
Aureliano Toso

Oriente, 1952

Two vases from the *Oriente* series. This series included the use of irregular multicolored patches of *avventurina* and canes of *zanfirico* and *reticello*, and generally were decorated with a white and aubergine pinwheel *murrine*.
14" high (cm. 36)
8.25" high (cm. 21)

Exhibitions:
1952, Venice, 26th Biennale Internazionale d'Arte.

Bibliography and comparative texts:
Mille anni..., 1982, n. 615;
Intérieurs'50, 1983, n. 137;
W. Neuwirth, 1987, n. 95;
M. Heiremans, 1989, n. 136;
R. Barovier Mentasti, 1992, n. 104;
M. Heiremans, 1993, nn. 155, 157, 161, 162;
M. Barovier, 1994, nn. 27, 28, 29;
Venezia e la Biennale..., 1995, n. 486;
F. Deboni, 1996, nn. 152, 153.

M. Heiremans, 1996, nn. 122, 123, 124;
Italienisches..., 1996, nn. 203, 204, 205, 206;
L.M. Barbero, 1997, p. 231;
M. Barovier, 1999, p. 217.

Vases from the *Oriente* series; photo from the archives.

112. Flavio Poli
Seguso Vetri D'Arte

Valva, 1954

A sculptural vase shaped like a clam shell composed of transparent grey glass *sommerso* in *cristallo*.
18" high (cm. 43)

Exhibitions:
1954, Venice, 27th Biennale Internazionale d'Arte.

Bibliography and comparative texts:
Domus, September, 1954;
R. Aloi, 1955, p.2;
G. Mariacher, 1967, p. 141;
R. Barovier Mentasti, 1977, n. 136;
Mille anni..., 1982, n. 639;
Die funfziger..., 1984, n. 10;
W. Neuwirth, 1987, n. 223;
La verrerie..., 1988, nn. 1, 6;
M. Heiremans, 1989, n. 113;
The Venetians..., 1989, n. 45;
M. Barovier, R. Barovier Mentasti,

A. Dorigato, 1995, n. 112;
M. Heiremans, 1996, n. 120;
Italienisches..., 1996, n. 13;
M. Barovier, 1999, p. 209.

Valve published in *Vetri d'oggi*, 1955.

113. Archimede Seguso
Vetreria Archimede Seguso

Composizione Lattimo, 1954

Vase in *cristallo* glass with the lower portion decorated with *a mezza filigrana* canes.
13.5" high (cm. 34)

Exhibitions:
1954, Venice, 27th Biennale Internazionale d'Arte.

Bibliography and comparative texts:
G. Mariacher, 1967, p. 135;
R. Barovier Mentasti, 1982, n. 311;
Mille anni..., 1982, n. 625;
M. Heiremans, 1989, n. 109;
U. Franzoi, 1991, nn. 26, 87, 88, 89, 90;
M. Heiremans, 1993, nn. 122, 123;
M. Barovier, R. Barovier Mentasti,
A. Dorigato, 1995, n. 119;
Venezia e la Biennale..., 1995, n. 484;
F. Deboni, 1996, n. 129;
M. Heiremans, 1996, n. 147;

Italienisches..., 1996, nn. 185, 186.

Works by Archimede Seguso at the 28th Biennale Internazionale d'Arte, Venice, 1954.

114. Archimede Seguso
Vetreria Archimede Seguso

Merletto, 1952

A tall vase composed of transparent straw-colored glass, decorated with *lattimo* threads obtained from *zanfirico* canes.
15.75" high (cm. 40)

Exhibitions:
1952, Venice, 26th Biennale Internazionale d'Arte.

Bibliography and comparative texts:
G. Mariacher, 1967, p. 138;
Mostra del Vetro..., 1963;
U. Franzoi, 1991, nn. 21, 48;
M. Barovier, 1994, n. 31;
M. Heiremans, 1996, n. 131;
I merletti..., 1999, p. 10.

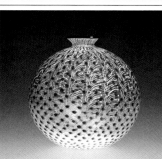

115. Archimede Seguso
Vetreria Archimede Seguso

Merletto Puntiforme, 1954

A globular vase composed of transparent glass and decorated with threads of *merletto lattimo* with the addition of controlled *puntini* (spots) of amethyst glass. Amethyst lip wrap.
9.5" high (cm. 24)

Bibliography and comparative texts:
U. Franzoi, 1991, nn. 22, 86;
R. Barovier Mentasti, 1995, n. 39;
F. Deboni, 1996, n. 130;
Italienisches..., 1996, n. 180;
I merletti..., 1999, p. 11.

116. Archimede Seguso
Vetreria Archimede Seguso

Polveri, 1953

A vase with three apertures composed of translucent amethyst glass with inclusions of gold leaf. This vase belongs to the *polveri* (powders) series.
9" high (cm. 23)

Bibliography and comparative texts:
M. Heiremans, 1989, n. 98.

117. Archimede Seguso
Vetreria Archimede Seguso

Ritorto a coste, 1950

Vase in translucent red glass with twisted ribbing and inclusions of gold leaf.
11" high (cm. 28)

Bibliography and comparative texts:
U. Franzoi, 1991, n. 35.

118. Archimede Seguso
Vetreria Archimede Seguso

Sfumato, 1954

A vessel in transparent red glass with one large aperture, two side lips and a stylized handle; inclusions of gold leaf throughout.
11.5" high (cm. 29)

Bibliography and comparative texts:
R. Barovier Mentasti, 1995a, n. 3.

119. Ermanno Toso
Fratelli Toso

Murrine spiraliformi, 1960-1962

Bowl composed of green, blue and yellow spiraled *murrine*.
Paper label: *Murano Glass Made in Italy*.
6" high (cm. 14)

Exhibitions:
1962, Venice, 31st Biennale Internazionale d'Arte;
1963, Venice, Exhibition of Murano Glass, Opera Bevilacqua la Masa.

Bibliography and comparison texts:
Mostra del vetro..., 1963;
M. Heiremans, 1989, nn. 158, 159;
M. Barovier, R. Barovier Mentasti, A. Dorigato, 1995, p. 141;
F. Deboni, 1996, n. 170;
M. Heiremans, 1996, n. 219;
M. Barovier, 1999, p. 258.

120. Ermanno Toso
Fratelli Toso

Kiku, 1959-1960

A glass vase of aubergine and *lattimo* pinwheel *murrine*, most of which have a red core.
7" high (cm. 18)

Bibliography and comparative texts:
M. Heiremans, 1989, nn. 163, 164.

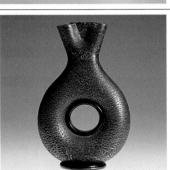

121. Ercole Barovier
Barovier & Toso

Barbarico, 1951

A footed vessel with one large aperture and a pinched mouth. The rough gold surface of the cobalt blue glass vessel, *colorazione a caldo senza fusione*.
11" high (cm. 27)

Exhibitions:
1951, Milan, 9th Triennale;
1952, Venice, 26th Biennale Internazionale d'Arte.

Bibliography and comparative texts:
Domus, 1951, October;
R. Aloi, 1952, n. 25;
A. Dorigato, 1989, n. 82;
M. Heiremans, 1989, n. 35;
The Venetians..., 1989, n. 35;
L'arte del vetro..., 1992, n. 374;
M. Barovier, 1993, n. 132;
M. Heiremans, 1993, n. 43;
M. Barovier, R. Barovier Mentasti, A. Dorigato, 1995, n. 92;

F. Deboni, 1996, n. 41;
Italienisches..., 1996, n. 258;
Il vetro italiano..., 1998, n. 101;
M. Barovier, 1999, p. 195.

Vessels from the *Barbarici* series; photo from the Barovier & Toso archives, 1951.

122. Ercole Barovier
Barovier & Toso

Barbarico, 1951

A small bowl. The rough gold surface of the cobalt blue glass is *colorazione a caldo senza fusione.*
6" high (cm. 15)

Exhibitions:
1951, Milan, 9th Triennale;
1952, Venice, 26th Biennale Internazionale d'Arte.

Bibliography and comparative texts:
Domus, 1951, October;
R. Aloi, 1952, n. 25;
A. Dorigato, 1989, n. 82;
M. Heiremans, 1989, n. 35;
The Venetians..., 1989, n. 35;
L'arte del vetro..., 1992, n. 374;
M. Barovier, 1993, n. 132;
M. Heiremans, 1993, n. 43;
M. Barovier, R. Barovier Mentasti, A. Dorigato, 1995, n. 92;

F. Deboni, 1996, n. 41;
Italienisches..., 1996, n. 258;
Il vetro italiano..., 1998, n. 101;
M. Barovier, 1999, p. 195.

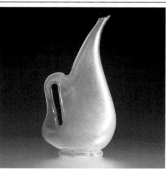

123. Ercole Barovier
Barovier & Toso

Eugeneo, 1951

A footed vessel with a vertical aperture to create a handle. Composed of strongly iridized pearl-colored glass, the surface coloring was *colorazione a caldo senza fusione.*
14.5" high (cm. 37)

Exhibitions:
1952, Venice, 26th Biennale Internazionale d'Arte.

Bibliography and comparative texts:
B. Nerozzi, 1987, n. 66;
A. Dorigato, 1989, nn. 80, 81;
M. Heiremans, 1989, n. 40;
The Venetians..., 1989, n. 35;
R. Barovier Mentasti, 1992, n. 86;
L'arte del vetro..., 1992, n. 373;
M. Barovier, 1993, n. 129;
M. Barovier, R. Barovier Mentasti, A. Dorigato, 1995, n. 93;
F. Deboni, 1996, n. 43;
Italienisches..., 1996, n. 259.

Vessels from the *Eugenei* series; photo from Marino Barovier archives.

124. Ercole Barovier
Barovier & Toso

Neolitico, 1954

A globular footed glass vase. The brown festoon decoration is obtained through *colorazione a caldo senza fusione.*
8" high (cm. 20)

Bibliography and comparative texts:
R. Aloi, 1955, p. 42;
W. Neuwirth, 1987, n. 85;
A. Dorigato, 1989, n. 86;
M. Heiremans, 1989, n. 41;
M. Barovier, 1993, n. 136.

125. Ercole Barovier
Barovier & Toso

Striati, 1954

Two tall glass vessels. The vessel on the left is composed of intersecting *cristallo* and aquamarine canes; the vessel one the right is composed of intersecting *cristallo* and amethyst canes.
16" high (cm. 41)
14" high (cm. 36)

Bibliography and comparative texts:
R. Aloi, 1955, p. 36;
A. Dorigato, 1989, p. 139.

Vessels from the *Striati* series published in *Vetri d'oggi, 1955.*

126. Ercole Barovier
Barovier & Toso

Pezzato, 1956

Glass vessel composed of red and *lattimo* patches *sommersi* in opaline glass.
10" high (cm. 25)

Bibliography and comparative texts:
A. Dorigato, 1989, p. 139;
M. Heiremans, 1989, n. 52;
M. Barovier, 1993, n. 144;
F. Deboni, 1996, n. 53;
M. Heiremans, 1996, nn. 160, 161.

127. Ercole Barovier
Barovier & Toso

A spina, 1958

Glass vase composed of green, *cristallo*, and amethyst glass patches arranged in a herringbone pattern.
9" high (cm. 23)

Exhibitions:
1958, Venice, 29th Biennale
Internazionale d'Arte.

Bibliography and comparative texts:
W. Neuwirth, 1987, n. 88;
A. Dorigato, 1989, n. 95;
M. Heiremans, 1989, n. 55;
The Venetians..., 1989, n. 40;
M. Barovier, 1993, n. 153;
R. Barovier Mentasi, 1994, n. 44;
M. Barovier, R. Barovier Mentasti,
A. Dorigato, 1995, n. 129;
F. Deboni, 1996, n. 47;
Italienisches..., 1996, n. 263.

128. Ercole Barovier
Barovier & Toso

Intarsio, 1961-1963

Vase composed of grey and red triangular shaped transparent glass patches *sommersi* in *cristallo*.
12" high (cm. 30)

Exhibitions:
1962, Venice, 31st Biennale
Internazionale d'Arte.

Bibliography and comparative texts:
Catalogue 31st Biennale..., 1962,
n. 212; G. Mariacher, 1967, p. 105;
R. Barovier Mentasti, 1977, n. 11;
A. Dorigato, 1989, nn. 106, 107;
M. Heiremans, 1989, n. 67;
H. Ricke, 1990, n. 384;
R. Barovier Mentasti, 1992, n. 139;
L'arte del vetro..., 1992, n. 374;
M. Barovier, 1993, nn. 165, 166, 167;
M. Heiremans, 1993, n. 55;
R. Barovier Mentasti, 1994, n. 64;

F. Deboni, 1996, n. 54;
Italienisches..., 1996, n. 270;
M. Barovier, 1999, pp. 238, 239.

129. Ercole Barovier
Barovier & Toso

Caccia, 1962

Cylindrical vase composed of two alternating glass bands. One band is made of circular *cristallo*, *lattimo* and blue *tessere*, the other is Diamond-shaped *cristallo* and black *tessere*.
9" high (cm. 23)

Exhibitions:
1962, Venice, 31st Biennale
Internazionale d'Arte.

Bibliography and comparative texts:
A. Dorigato, 1989, n. 108;
R. Barovier Mentasti, 1992, n. 139;
M. Barovier, 1993, n. 163;
R. Barovier Mentasti, 1994, n. 63;
F. Deboni, 1996, n. 50.

Vessels from the *Caccia* series, photo from the Barovier & Toso archives, 1962.

130. Ercole Barovier
Barovier & Toso

Tessere Policrome, 1962

Bowl composed of *cristallo tessere*. The top portion is a band of rectangular *tessere* outlined in aubergine; the lower portion is composed of circular *murrine* in red, *lattimo* and blue connected by an aubergine line.
Engraved: *Ercole Barovier 2/11/62*.
3.5" high (cm. 9)
17.5" Ø (cm. 19)

Bibliography and comparative texts:
M. Barovier, 1993, n. 164;
Italienisches..., 1996, n. 268.

131. Ercole Barovier
Barovier & Toso

Christian Dior, 1969

Stoppered bottle in a Scottish plaid pattern. The design was achieved by intersecting canes of blue and *cristallo* glass with canes of green and *cristallo*.
Engraved: *Christian Dior*.
9.75" high (cm. 25)

Bibliography and comparative texts:
M. Barovier, 1993, n. 177;
F. Deboni, 1996, n. 57;
Italienisches..., 1996, n. 269.

132. Ercole Barovier
Barovier & Toso

Rotellato, 1970

A footed vase composed of circular *tessere a dentelli* (with indentations) in *cristallo*, blue and red glass.
11" high (cm. 28)

Exhibitions:
1970, Venice, 35th Biennale Internazionale d'Arte.

Bibliography and comparative texts:
A. Dorigato, 1989, n. 117;
M. Barovier, 1993, nn. 178, 179;
M. Barovier, R. Barovier Mentasti, A. Dorigato 1995, n. 184;
F. Deboni, 1996, n. 50;
M. Heiremans, 1996, n. 255;
M. Barovier, 1999, p. 277.

133. Alfredo Barbini
Vetreria Alfredo Barbini

Vetro pesante, 1962

Sculptural vessel in *pesante* (heavy) glass, *sommerso* in several layers of glass. The core of the sculpture is red, the finish a tight wheel-carved horizontal *inciso*.
10.25" high (cm. 26)

Exhibitions:
1962, Venice, 31st Biennale Internazionale d'Arte.

Bibliography and comparative texts:
Catalogue 31st Biennale..., 1962, n. 210;
Mille anni..., 1982, n. 571;
M. Heiremans, 1989, n. 30;
M. Heiremans, 1993, n. 17;
M. Barovier, R. Barovier Mentasti, A. Dorigato, 1995, n. 134;
M. Heiremans, 1996, n. 213;
Italienisches..., 1996, n. 252;
M. Barovier, 1999, p. 243.

134. Ludovico Diaz de Santillana
Venini & C., Murano

Cannette, 1962

Vase in transparent amethyst glass decorated with applied canes of green glass.
Acid stamped: *venini murano ITALIA*.
10" high (cm. 25)

Exhibitions:
1963, Venice, Exhibition of Murano glass, Opera Bevilacqua La Masa.

Bibliography and comparative texts:
Mostra del vetro..., 1963;
M. Heiremans, 1989, n. 217;
F. Deboni, 1989, n. 169;
Gli Artisti..., 1996, n. 234.

Vases from the *Cannette* series, published in the catalogue of the Mostra del vetro di Murano, 1963.

135. Venini & C.

A murrine, 1960

A plate with the center composed of green *murrine*, the outer rim composed of green and aubergine *murrine* surrounding a band of blue *murrine*. This plate is part of a series of *murrine* objects created in the 1960s by the design studio of Venini. The designer is unknown.
10.25" Ø (cm. 26)

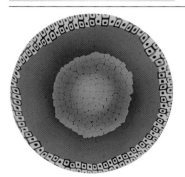

136. Venini & C.

A murrine, 1960

Plate made with *lattimo* and amethyst *tessere*, part of a series of *murrine* objects created in the 1960s by the design studio of Venini. The designer is unknown.
9" Ø (cm. 23)

Bibliography and comparative texts:
The Venetians..., 1989, n. 31.

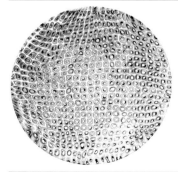

137. Tobia Scarpa
Venini & C.

Occhi, 1960-1961

A vase composed of alternating
pasta vitrea murrine, black with a
cristallo core and red with a *cristallo*
core.
13" high (cm. 31)

Exhibitions:
1960, Milan, 12th Triennale;
1962, Venice, 31st Biennale
Internazionale d'Arte.

Bibliography and comparative texts:
Venini grey catalogue, n. 8526;
Domus, 1960, October, p. 166;
W. Neuwirth, 1987, n. 171;
La Verrerie..., 1988, n. 2;
F. Deboni, 1989, nn. 164, 165;
The Venetians..., 1989, n. 18;
H. Ricke, 1990, n. 379;
R. Barovier Mentasti, 1992, n. 102;
L'arte del vetro, 1992, n. 363;
M. Heiremans, 1993, n. 240;

M. Barovier, 1994, n. 43;
M. Barovier, R. Barovier Mentasti,
A. Dorigato, 1995, n. 147;
F. Deboni, 1996, n. 224;
Gli Artisti..., 1996, nn. 219, 220, 221;
Italienisches..., 1996, nn. 153, 154;
M. Barovier, 1999, p. 261.

Vases from the *Occhi* series.

138. Tobia Scarpa
Venini & C.

Cinese, 1960 ca.

An anthracite black Chinese ginger
jar shaped vessel with a matching
lid. The entire vessel is heavily
iridized.
Acid stamped: *venini murano ITALIA.*
10" high (cm. 25)

139. Thomas Stearns
Venini & C.

Nebbia lunare, 1962

Mist of the moon vessel in
transparent glass. The lower portion
is cased in heavily iridized dark blue
glass, the top portion in clear glass is
inciso with fine vertical cuts. The two
portions are separated by an *inciso*
asymmetrical band.
Acid stamped: *venini murano ITALIA.*
4.5" high (cm. 10)

Bibliography and comparative texts:
Domus, 1963, July, p. 40;
M. Heiremans, 1993, n. 242;
M. Heiremans, 1996, nn. 204, 205;
Italienisches..., 1996, nn. 159, 160.

Nebbia Lunare published in the July,
1963 issue of *Domus*.

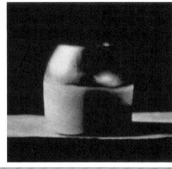

140. Thomas Stearns
Venini & C.

Sentinella di Venezia, 1962

A multicolored sculpture composed
of iridescent glass canes, *murrine*
and some vertical *inciso* work. One
of two existing examples.
Engraved: *T. Stearns 62 Venini
Sentinella di Venezia version #1.*
20.5" high (cm. 52)

Exhibitions:
1962, Venice, 31st Biennale
Internazionale d'Arte.

Bibliography and comparative texts:
The Venetians..., 1989, n. 55.

Venini display at the 31st Biennale
Internazionale d'Arte, Venice, 1962.

141. Thomas Stearns
Venini & C.

Cappello del Doge, 1962

A double *incalmo* asymmetrical
vessel in yellow, *cristallo* and green
glass with a strongly iridized surface.
Acid stamped: *venini murano ITALIA.*
5.5" high (cm. 14)

Exhibitions:
1962, Venice, 31st Biennale
Internazionale d'Arte.

Bibliography and comparative texts:
Domus, January, 1962, p. 38;
Domus, July, 1963, p. 40;
F. Deboni, 1989, n. 170;
R. Barovier Mentasti, 1992, n. 141;
M. Barovier, R. Barovier Mentasti,
A. Dorigato, 1995, n. 149;
Venezia e la Biennale..., 1995, n. 567;
F. Deboni, 1996, n. 227;
Gli Artisti..., 1996, n. 223;
M. Heiremans, 1996, n. 202;
Italienisches..., 1996, n. 158.

Venini display at the 31st Biennale
Internazionale d'Arte, Venice, 1962.

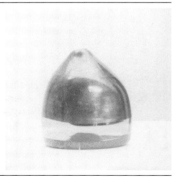

142. Thomas Srearn
Venini & C.

Il vaso per le lacrime del Doge, 1961

Green Orb. A vessel for the Doge's tears. A prototype composed of horizontal green glass canes with an inlay of silver and gold at the aperture.
Engraved: *Stearns per Venini 61 Il vaso per le lacrime del Doge Orbe verde.*
Hand made label: *Stearns Venini 61 - Vessel for The Doges Tears.*
5.5" high (cm. 14)

Venini display at the 31st Biennale Internazionale d'Arte, Venice, 1962.

143. Peter Pelzel and Alessandro Pianon
Vetreria Vistosi

Pulcini, 1960-1961

Seven glass birds standing on metal legs. The bodies are in transparent or translucent glass decorated with *murrine* or multicolored glass canes. The orange bird on the left, decorated with glass *granzeoli*, was designed by Peter Pelzel, the others by Alessandro Pianon.

8" high (cm. 20)
8" high (cm. 20)
6" high (cm. 16)
7" high (cm. 18)
11" high (cm. 28)
12.5" high (cm. 32)
6" high (cm. 16)

Bibliography and comparative texts:
Domus, 1962, April;
B. Nerozzi, 1987, nn. 130, 131, 132, 133;
M. Heiremans, 1989, nn. 230, 231;
The Venetians..., 1989, n. 36;
R. Barovier Mentasti, 1992, n. 119;
M. Heiremans, 1993, n. 249;
F. Deboni, 1996, n. 243;

M. Heiremans, 1996, nn. 209, 211;
M. Barovier, 1996, n. 103;
M. Barovier, 1999, p. 275.

Pulcini, *Domus*, April, 1962.

144. Anzolo Fuga
Aureliano Toso

Fiori, 1968 ca.

Six flowers in transparent glass decorated with *murrine* and multicolored glass canes.
The flowers sit on metal bases that emulate leaves and stems.
These flowers are prototypes and were never produced.

15.5" high (cm. 39)
15" high (cm. 38)
16" high (cm. 41)
18.5" high (cm. 47)
14" high (cm. 36)
15" high (cm. 38)

145. Tapio Wirkkala
Venini & C.

Bolle, 1966

Five multicolored *Incalmo* bottle-shaped vases.
Engraved: *venini ITALIA TW.*
6.75" high (cm. 17)
9" high (cm. 23)
18.2" high (cm. 47)
12" high (cm. 30)
8" high (cm. 20)

Bibliography and comparative texts:
Domus, 1968, February;
G. Mazzotti, T. Carta, 1971, p. 155, n.c.;
Venezianisches..., 1981, n. 40;
Murano Oggi, 1981, nn. 514, 515, 516;
R. Barovier Mentasti, 1992, n. 322;
Mille anni..., 1982, n. 653;
G. Duplani Tucci, 1989,
nn. 46, 47, 48, 49;
M. Heiremans, 1989, n. 221;
Gli Artisti..., 1996, n. 238;
Venini Venezia, 1998, p. 77;
M. Barovier, 1999, p. 271.

146. Benjamin Moore
Venini & C.

Tessuto ad incalmo, 1979

Incalmo vase. The upper portion is composed of a spiraling *tessuto* of pink, green and black canes of glass, the lower in black glass.
Engraved: *Benjamin Moore Venini.*
10" high (cm. 25),
10" Ø (cm. 25)

Bibliography and comparative texts:
Gli Artisti..., 1989, n. 249;
M. Barovier, 1999, p. 289.

147. James Carpenter
Venini & C.

Vetro Tessuto, 1979 ca.

A cylindrical vase composed of diagonal patches of glass *tessuto* made of *lattimo* and coral canes with black and coral alternating patches.
Engraved: *Carpenter Venini*.
10.75" high (cm. 27,5)

148. James Carpenter
Venini & C.

Prototipo, 1979 ca.

A prototype vessel composed of spiraling horizontal canes in turquoise green and black glass.
Engraved: *Carpenter, Venini*.
4.75" high (cm. 12)

Bibliography and comparative texts:
M. Barovier, 1999, p. 288.

149. James Carpenter
Venini & C.

Calabash, 1980

Three opaque glass vessels.
The one on the left is yellow with a jagged green and blue pattern outlined in red; the one in the middle is black with turquoise and red; the bowl on the right is white with green and yellow glass.
Engraved: *venini italia*.
8.25" high (cm. 21)
12" high (cm. 30,5)
5.75" high (cm. 14,5)

Bibliography and comparative texts:
Murano oggi..., 1981, nn. 331, 332;
G. Duplani Tucci, 1989, p. 93;
Gli Artisti..., 1996, n. 251;
M. Barovier, 1999, p. 319.

150. James Carpenter
Venini & C.

Calabash, 1980

An opaque yellow glass plate decorated with a spiraling pattern of red and turquoise glass canes.
Engraved: *venini italia*.
11" Ø (cm. 28)

Bibliography and comparative texts:
Murano oggi..., 1981, nn. 331, 332;
Duplani Tucci, 1989, p. 93;
Gli Artisti..., 1996, n. 251;
M. Barovier, 1999, p. 319.

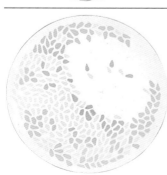

151. Laura Diaz de Santillana
Venini & C.

Glicine, 1979

A plate with *cristallo*, yellow, amethyst and blue pale *murrine* arranged to replicate a wisteria pattern.
Engraved: *venini italia 79 100/3 Laura*.
10.5" Ø (cm. 26,5)

Bibliography and comparative texts:
Gli Artisti..., 1996, n. 255.

152. Alessandro Diaz de Santillana
Venini & C.

Coccio, 1983

A white vase composed of *lattimo murrine* decorated with an abstract pattern in black, and finished with applications of gold leaf.
6.25" high. (cm. 16)

Bibliography and comparative texts:
Gli Artisti..., 1996, n. 261;
Venini Venezia, 1998, p. 79.

153. Toots Zynsky
Venini & C.

Chiacchere, 1984

Two vases also entitled *Mulinello*. The one on the left is composed of pink glass cased in blue with pink mouth and applied green threads. The one on the right is in black glass cased in green with black mouth and applied black threads.
Engraved: *Zinsky x Venini 1984*.
10" high (cm. 26,5)
14" high (cm. 35,5)

Bibliography and comparative texts:
G. Duplani Tucci, 1989, n. 67;
R. Barovier Mentasti, 1992, n. 163;
Glas Band II, 1992, p. 128;
Gli Artisti..., 1996, n. 263.

154. Toots Zynsky
Venini & C.

Folto, 1984

A bowl composed of cased blue glass decorated with an irregular application of pink threads.
Engraved: *Zinsky x Venini 1984*.
5" high (cm. 12,5)

Bibliography and comparative texts:
Gli Artisti..., 1996, n. 262;
M. Barovier, 1999, p. 317.

155. Toots Zynsky
Venini & C.

Folto, 1984

A turquoise bowl cased in *lattimo* glass decorated with a random design of pink and pale blue threads.
Engraved: *Zinsky x Venini 1984*.
7.25" high. (cm. 18,5)

Bibliography and comparative texts:
Gli Artisti..., 1996, n. 263;
M. Barovier, 1999, p. 317.

156. Toots Zynsky
Venini & C.

Folto, 1984

A green vase decorated with a random design of orange threads.
Engraved: *Zinsky x Venini 1984*.
12.5" high. (cm. 31,5)

Bibliography and comparative texts:
Gli Artisti..., 1996, n. 262;
M. Barovier, 1999, p. 317.

157. Lino Tagliapietra

Boats, 1998

Two boats. The one on the top is composed of horizontal white glass canes, the other with multicolored canes. Both are finished with a dense and regular wheel-carved *battitura*.
77" (cm. 195)
73" (cm. 185)

Exhibitions:
1998, Venice, Venezia Aperto Vetro.

Bibliography and comparative texts:
International New Glass..., 1998, p. 128;
M. Barovier, 1998a, pp. 14, 15, 100, 101;
M. Barovier, 1999, p. 390, 391.

158. Yoichi Ohira

Polveri, 1997

Two vessels from the *Polveri* series. The one on the right is composed of turquoise and ruby glass canes and red *polveri* (dust), the other is salmon with red glass canes and pink *polveri*. The surface of both vases is finished with a fine *velato* executed at the wheel in the *moleria*.
Engraved: *Yoichi Ohira m. L. Serena 1/1 unico 4.11.1997 Murano.*
4.125" high (cm. 10,5)

Engraved: *Yoichi Ohira m. L. Serena 1/1 unico 29.10.1997 Murano.*
6.5" high (cm. 17)

Bibliography and comparative texts:
A. Dorigato, 1998, pp. 60, 61;

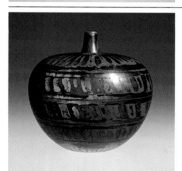

159. Yoichi Ohira

Pasta vitrea, 1997

A vessel composed of transparent turquoise glass and opaque red *pasta vitrea*.
Engraved: *Yoichi Ohira m. L. Serena 1/1 unico 20.11.1997 Murano.*
6.5" high (cm. 17)

Bibliography and comparative texts:
A. Dorigato, 1998, pp. 60, 61;

160. Yoichi Ohira

Pasta vitrea, 1997

Left to Right:
A bi-colored vessel. One half composed of light wood grained colored glass canes with red and *cristallo murrine*, the other half of a dark wood-grained colored glass with turquoise and *cristallo* and yellow and *cristallo murrine*.
Engraved: *Yoichi Ohira m. L. Serena 1/1 unico 20.06.1997 Murano.*
5.5" high (cm. 14)

A vase composed of opaque mustard-colored glass and decorated with opaque red *pasta vitrea*. Engraved: *Yoichi Ohira m. L. Serena 1/1 unico 16.04.1997 Murano.*
6.25" high (cm. 16)

A vessel composed of transparent turquoise glass and decorated with opaque patches of light and dark brown *pasta vitrea* to create a mosaic decor.
Engraved: *Yoichi Ohira m. L. Serena 1/1 unico 01.06.1998 Murano.*
7.5" high (cm. 19)

Finestre vessel composed of wood-colored glass canes with windows of transparent turquoise green glass. Surface finished with a fine *velato* executed in the *moleria*.
Engraved: *Yoichi Ohira m. L. Serena 1/1 unico 21.04.1998 Murano.*
6.5" high (cm. 17)

Exhibitions:
1998, Venice, Museo Correr.

Bibliography and comparative texts:
A. Dorigato, 1998, pp. 28, 32, 45, 47.

161. Yoichi Ohira

Fiori verdi e blu, 1998
Pasta Vitrea, 1998

The vase on the left is composed of green, blue and brown glass canes inlaid with *murrine*.
Engraved: *Yoichi Ohira m. L. Serena 1/1 unico 06.10.1998 Murano.*
7.5" high (cm. 19,5)

The vase on the right is composed of *lattimo* glass canes and transparent glass inlaid with *murrine*.
Engraved: *Yoichi Ohira m. L. Serena 1/1 unico 02.04.1998 Murano.*
8.25" high (cm. 21,5)

162. Yoichi Ohira

Metamorfosi, 1999

A vessel composed of *lattimo* glass canes with inlays of *cristallo murrine*. The surface is finished with a fine *velato*.
Engraved: *Yoichi Ohira m. L. Serena 1/1 unico 1999 Murano*.
10" high (cm. 25,5)

Exhibitions:
1999, Venice, Venezia Aperto Vetro.

Bibliography and comparative texts:
M. Barovier, 1999, p. 369.

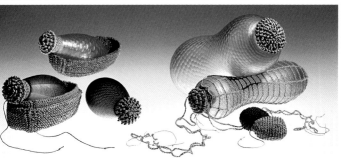

163. Cristiano Bianchin

Nidi, semi e fusi, 1996

A grouping of five *nidi*, *semi* and *fusi* resting in or among baskets.
All glass pieces are transparent aubergine, clear or straw colored.
The surfaces are *battuto* with applied gold leaf throughout.
The *corolle*, baskets, and other elements are hand woven in hemp by the artist.

13" long (cm. 33)
13" long (cm. 33)
8" long (cm. 20)
8" long (cm. 20)
8" long (cm. 20)

Exhibitions:
1996, Venice, Venezia Aperto Vetro;
1998, Venice, Venezia Aperto Vetro.

Bibliography and comparative texts:
International New Glass, 1996, p. 101;
International New Glass, 1998, p. 59.

164. Laura Diaz de Santillana

T5 L'occhio, 1999

Sculpture in opaque amber glass.
The *occhio* (eye) in the center is in transparent turquoise glass.
Engraved: *Laura de Santillana*.
8.75" x 7.5" x 1.4"
(cm. 22 x 19.2 x 3,6)

165. Laura Diaz de Santillana

T15, 1999

A sculpture composed of translucent red glass.
Engraved: *Laura de Santillana*.
20" x 8.75" x 1.5"
(cm. 50 x 22 x 4)

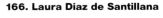

166. Laura Diaz de Santillana

S3, S4, S2, 1999

Three black glass rectangular sculptures. The ones in the left and center have a turquoise blue edge, the one on the right amber.
Engraved: *Laura de Santillana*.
12.5" x 8.75" x 1.5"
(cm. 31 x 22 x 4)
10.75" x 8.75" x 1.5"
(cm. 27 x 22 x 4)
12.5" x 8.75" x 1.5"
(cm. 31 x 22 x 4)

Artists

Alfredo Barbini
(1912)

Glassblower, designer and entrepreneur, Alfredo Barbini was born in Murano and began working with glass while very young.
At seventeen and a half, following a brief apprenticeship, he became a glass *maestro*; first at the Cristalleria Franchetti and then at the S.A.I.A.R. Ferro Toso. After 1932, he worked at the Zecchin-Martinuzzi furnace with the sculptor Napoleone Martinuzzi, and began a collaboration which would last through 1936. This would prove to be fundamental to his artistic development, especially in regard to sculpture in solid *massiccio* glass. In 1937, he became a partner at V.A.M.S.A. and was the *primo maestro* of the main team of the furnace continuing his experimentation with thick glass and executing works designed by the artists Ermenegildo Ripa and Luigi Scarpa Croce. In 1946, he became partner and artistic director of the new furnace, Gino Cenedese & C. With this furnace, he participated in the 1948 Biennale di Venezia exhibiting a remarkable series of sculptures in *corroso* glass such as *Torso* and *Collasso*. In 1950, he opened his own furnace, Vetreria Alfredo Barbini, where he continues, until today, to experiment with the sculptural qualities of glass using materials and forms that are more and more essential. This can seen in his series *Pesci* and *Tulipani* or in the *Vetri Pesanti* of the early 60s. Assisted by his son, Flavio, since 1968, Barbini still works as *maestro* and artistic director of the furnace he created in 1950.

Benvenuto Barovier
(1855-1932)

Maestro and designer
Benvenuto Barovier first worked as a glassblower for a company called Compagnia di Venezia e Murano (C.V.M.) where he was noted for his remarkable manual skills. In 1877, he and his brother, Giuseppe, were invited by Antonio Salviati to collaborate in his new furnace called Salviati dott. Antonio. When Salviati retired from the business of production in 1883, Benvenuto and Giuseppe bought the company where they worked as glassblowers and designers, eventually renaming it Artisti Barovier after Salviati's death in 1890. Among Benvenuto's many creations are some extraordinary pieces made in *mosaico* glass. Apart from the significant technical quality of these objects, one can perceive the passionate experimentation carried out by the *maestro* from Murano, who frequently used crushed glass to decorate his pieces. He and his brother received widespread critical acclaim at several exhibitions that took place at Cà Pesaro. After the transformation of the company into Vetreria Artistica Barovier & C. (1919), Benvenuto Barovier continued to participate actively in the furnace.

Ercole Barovier
(1889-1974)

Entrepreneur and designer, Ercole Barovier was the son of Benvenuto Barovier. At age 30, he became a partner in his father's company, the Vetreria Artistica Barovier & C. After becoming its artistic director in 1926, he took over its management with his brother. He became sole proprietor in 1936, engineering the fusion between his own glass workshop and the S.A.I.A.R. Ferro-Toso. In 1942, the new company was renamed Barovier & Toso and Ercole maintained artistic direction of the new company until 1972. Over the course of his 50-year activity, he invented numerous decorative techniques which contributed significantly to the renovation of art glass. His first major successes date back to the 20s; first with the *murrine* vessels, then with totally original creations such as the *Primavera* glass collection of 1929-30. After the 30s, he dedicated himself entirely to experimenting with new multi-colored effects. In addition he perfected the *colorazione a caldo senza fusione* which he first used in 1935-36 to create the series *Crepuscolo*, *Autunno Gemmato*, *Marina Gemmata* and *Laguna Gemmata*. Before World War II, he preferred soft shapes and rather thick materials, whereas in the post-war period his interest turned specifically to the field of traditional techniques, which he continued to reinterpret through his very last creations with the series, *A Tessere*, in 1972. In the 50s, his work distinguished itself both for the vivid quality of its colors as well as for the singularity of the materials noted for the rawness of their surfaces like the *barbarici*. In addition, series like the *Eugenei* and *Aborigeni* were singled out for the primitive inspiration of their shapes. During the 60s and 70s, he gave new interpretations of his *a tessere* glass with the *Dorici*, *Caccia*, *Rotellati* and other series which were characterized by unusual color combinations.

Giuseppe Barovier
(1853-1942)

Giuseppe Barovier went to work at the Compagnia di Venezia e Murano at a very young age and soon, due to his exceptional skills, became a *maestro*. He distinguished himself in various fields from the decoration of blown pieces to the execution of *murrine* glass, to chandeliers. In 1877, he left the Compagnia di Venezia e Murano to follow Antonio Salviati to his new glass workshop called Salviati dott. Antonio, where he worked with his brother Benvenuto. After the Barovier's family took over the ownership of the furnace in 1883, renaming it Artisti Barovier in 1890, Giuseppe became *maestro* and designer with his brother. Among his many creations that deserve mention are his refined *murrine*, which the Artisti Barovier presented at the Cà Pesaro exhibitions. When Artisti Barovier was liquidated in 1919, he, his brother Benvenuto, and their sons founded the Vetreria Artistica Barovier & C., where he worked until the end of the 20s.

Nicolò Barovier
(1895-1947)

The son of Benvenuto Barovier, Nicolò was both an entrepreneur and a designer. He and his brother Ercole, joined the Vetreria Artistica Barovier & C. in 1919 as partners and glass designers. After 1926, they both became managers of the company. His familiarity with contemporary painting led him to produce extraordinary *murrine* vessels, which can be recognized for their elaborate geometric patterns and their unique colors. From 1932 on, he shared ownership of Vetreria Artistica Barovier & C. with his brother Ercole. He worked actively in the glass workshop through 1936.

Cristiano Bianchin
(1963)

Born in Venice, where he lives and works, Cristiano Bianchin attended the Accademia di Belle Arti di Venezia where he studied under the direction of the renowned artist Emilio Vedova and graduated with a degree in painting in 1987. Since 1984, he has exhibited at public institutions and private galleries, and his first personal show was held at the Galleria Bevilacqua La Masa in 1987. As an emerging artist, Bianchin conceives his own artistic language as a reading of experimental poetics involving the possible exchange between the sensuality of seeing and the materials used in art. His first experiments in glass date from 1992 and have been presented in numerous collective and personal exhibitions, such as the one held in 1995 at the Museo Antonio Canova (also known as the Possagno) near Treviso. Bianchin views his work with glass having an evolutionary continuity based on the classical validity of glassblowing techniques which he confronts with the experimentation of new sculptural forms. His *Nidi* date from 1996: they are works conceived as mineral architectures whose surface is textured using the refined Murano glass techniques of *battitura* and *molatura*. Between 1998 and 1999, he created his *Riposapesi* in which the blown glass pieces, black or vividly colored, are synthetically austere. Bianchin was selected in 1995 and 1997 as the Italian artist at the Corning Museum of Glass in New York. He participated at *Aperto Vetro*, the International Exhibition of Contemporary Glass in Venice, in 1996 and 1998. His works have been acquired by prestigious public and private collections and have been published in books, catalogues and the most important art magazines.

Fulvio Bianconi
(1915-1996)

Fluvio Bianconi is a graphic artist, caricaturist, and designer. Born in Padua, he attended the Istituto d'Arte and the Accademia di Belle Arti in Venice. He first encountered glass at age fifteen when he studied decoration with enamels under the guidance of Michele Pinto. During the late 30s, he worked as a caricaturist, graphic artist and illustrator for various publishing houses such as Mondadori, Rizzoli, Garzanti, etc. After World War II, he came to Murano to study glass techniques and met Paolo Venini. A productive relationship ensued as he began a collaboration with Venini in 1947 that lasted through the entire decade of the 50s. One of his most characteristic works is the long series of stylized figurines which he designed at the end of the 40s, taking his inspiration from the Italian Commedia dell'Arte. His *pezzati* vessels proved extraordinary due to their richness in color, as were the *fazzoletti*, created with Venini himself, which where presented in several different textures. He obtained widespread acclaim for the *a Macchie* and *Fasce orrizontali* series in which Bianconi revealed a marked painterly vocation. In the 50s, he worked with other workshops such as the Vetreria Cenedese, designing vessels with applications and other pieces with cased decorations. From 1958 to 1961, he designed glass pieces for I.V.R. Mazzega. In 1963, he designed for the Vetreria Vistosi. And in 1967, he began working again with Venini, creating vessels with unusual shapes such as the *Informale* (1968). After another contact with Venini in 1989, he designed for De Majo from 1991 to 1992.

Tomaso Buzzi
(1900-1981)

Architect and designer, Tommaso Buzzi was born in Sondrio and graduated in Architecture at the Politecnico di Milano. In Milan, he worked in the field of architecture, interiors, graphic design, set design and applied arts. In 1927, he joined *Il Labirinto*, founded to "promote the spreading of modern decorative arts in the home", to which Paolo Venini, Gio Ponti, Carla Visconi di Modrone, Emilio Lancia and Pietro Chiesa also belonged. From 1932 to 1934, he was artistic director of Venini & C., for whom he designed a very refined series of works. They were characterized by the elegant *Novecento* styles in *lattimo* and opaque turquoise glass with black detailing and clear pieces with branch-like applications. Experimenting with traditional techniques, he also designed vessels and bowls with unusual colors. His best known series, his *Alba*, *Laguna* and *Alga*, are known for their pastel tones which were created by using several successive thin layers of glass and then a final application of gold leaf. After World War II, Buzzi concluded his experience with glass art and returned to his professional activity, dedicating himself to painting.

James Carpenter
(1949)

Born in Washington D.C, James Carpenter graduated in 1972 from the Rhode Island School of Design with a B.F.A in Sculpture. Carpenter first collaborated at Venini & C. from October 1971 to May 1972. He returned several times to participate in the design of various glassworks. During this time, he worked along with Ludovico Diaz de Santillana experimenting in new techniques for the creation of large multicolored glass windows. His designs were included in the exhibition of historical and contemporary Venini glass held in New York in 1984. Among the works he designed for Venini are the *Calabash*, executed with the use of multicolored glass rods. For more than 25 years, the work of sculptor James Carpenter has focused on the exploration of light as a means to bring form to structure and reveal the environment. As an artist considered to be a foremost innovator in materials technologies, Carpenter has worked collaboratively with major architects in the United States and abroad on significant building projects and has received many major architectural and public Art commissions. Currently James Carpenter works in New York.

Alessandro Diaz de Santillana
(1959)

Born in Paris of Venetian origin, Alessandro Diaz de Santillana graduated in Art History at the Università di Venezia in 1981. At the Venini & C., managed by his father, Ludovico Diaz de Santillana, he had the opportunity to meet many artists from the American Studio Glass movement who worked at the furnace thanks to the openness and generosity of the artistic director. He collaborated with Venini & C. through 1985, and later with Rosenthal and Eos. He has been exhibiting since 1985, after choosing to progressively dedicate himself to his own personal artistic development and to the creation of original works.

Laura Diaz de Santillana
(1955)

Born in Venice, Laura Diaz de Santillana attended the School of Visual Arts in New York. After working as a graphic designer at the design firm of Vignelli Associates in 1976, she returned to Italy and began an active collaboration with the Vetreria Venini & C. Her work at the furnace, managed with a spirit of great openness by her father Ludovico Diaz de Santillana, brought Laura Diaz de Santillana in close contact with the many Italian and foreign artists who came there in those years. During that period, she used the techniques of Murano to create refined works with unusual colors, among which the plates in *vetro mosaico* deserve particular mention. From 1985 to 1993, she was the designer and artistic director of Eos and later worked as designer for Rosenthal and for Ivan Baj. Further developing her own artistic identity through the creation of original works, lately she has focused her attention on the sculptural qualities of the material which is often finished in singular textures. De Santillana's meditated study of color has produced original solutions. She has participated in numerous exhibitions in Europe, the United States and Japan, winning widespread consensus. Several of her works have been acquired by public and private collections such as the Corning Museum of Glass, the Museum fur Kunst und Gewerbe in Hamburg, and the Museo Vetrario di Murano.

Ludovico Diaz de Santillana
(1931-1989)

Architect, designer and entrepreneur, Ludovico Diaz de Santillana was born in Rome. He graduated with a degree in Architecture in Venice and began his profession as architect and university professor. After the death of his father-in-law, Paolo Venini, in 1959, he took over the administrative and artistic direction of Venini & C. and remained in this position until 1985. Though he continued the production strategy already in place to a large degree, he increased the external collaborations with both well-known artists and young talents from abroad, especially from the United States. He himself designed important collections of blown vessels and *murrine* glass, as well as large lighting projects. After 1980, he was joined by his daughter, Laura, in the artistic direction of the company.

Giorgio Ferro
(1931)

Born in Murano the son of the glassmaker Galliano Ferro, Giorgio Ferro attended the Istituto d'Arte di Venezia, dedicating himself initially to painting. He soon went to work as a designer at the Vetreria A.V.E.M. where his father had become a partner after the death of its artistic director Giulio Radi (1952). His most significant work of the period is a piece called *Anse Volanti*, dark colored vessels with iridescent surfaces and ample handles obtained hot directly from the body which produces a remarkable sculptural effect. When his father, Galliano, left A.V.E.M. in 1955 to found his own company, he followed him to become the artistic director of the new furnace and designed thin blown pieces as well as essentially-shaped encased glass pieces. He has been the owner of Galliano Ferro since 1972.

Anzolo Fuga
(1915-1998)

Anzolo Fuga was born on Murano. He apprenticed as a draftsman at the Cristalleria di Venezia e Murano and attended the Istituto d'Arte di Venezia, where he studied under Guido Balsamo Stella. In 1954, he opened a shop for the decoration of blown glass and the art of stained-glass windows, and it is here that he began to use sheets of Murano glass blown and decorated in hot-work. His colorful stained glass windows were successfully exhibited in several editions of the Biennale. He was director of the Abate Zanetti school of art for glassworkers from 1949 through 1972, and he collaborated freelance with several workshops after the late 50s. Among them was A.V.E.M., for whom he created large pieces with asymmetric shapes and abstract decor using *murrine* and glass rods in almost all of his brightly colored collections. During this time, he also collaborated with Domus Vetri d'Arte and IVR Mazzega.

Dino Martens
(1894-1970)

Painter and designer, Dino Martens was born in Venice where he attended the Accademia di Belle Arti. In the mid 20s he moved to Murano, where, for a short time, he was a partner and decorator for the glass factory S.A.L.I.R. Later he worked as a designer for Salviati & C. and the Successori Andrea Rioda. His *Novecento* style paintings were exhibited at the Biennale di Venezia between 1924 and 1930. Upon his return from the African War in 1939, he became artistic director of the glass factory Aureliano Toso. From 1946 to 1960, Martens designed an incredible series of works for Toso. Using traditional Venetian techniques, he was able to obtain strikingly original multicolored effects combined with particularly daring asymmetric shapes. They included the compositions of glass rods called *Zanfirici*; colorful pieces composed with irregular shadings, and inserts of *avventurina* and rods of *filigrana* called *Oriente*; as well as the unusual shapes of the *Sommersi* with *battuto* finish and the inside cased with multicolored glass. His collaboration with the Aureliano Toso ended in 1963.

**Napoleone Martinuzzi
(1892-1977)**

The son of a glassblower from Murano, Napoleone Martinuzzi was a sculptor, designer and businessman. He attended the Accademia di Belle Arti di Venezia and after, joined the secessionist group of Cà Pesaro, where he exhibited his sculptures in 1908. His activity as a sculptor was intense in those years and he exhibited in the major Italian events as well as in Paris, Brussels and Vienna. From 1917 on, he was Gabriele D'Annunzio's favorite artist and he designed a funeral monument for him, as well as sculpture and many works in glass which may still be seen today at the Vittoriale. Between 1921 and 1931, he directed the Museo Vetrario di Murano and in 1925 he became a partner and artistic director at the Vetri Soffiati Muranesi Venini & C. After carrying on the concepts defined by his predecessor, Vittorio Zecchin, and creating beautifully transparent blown glass pieces, he elaborated on his own distinct style directly derived from his experience as a *Novecento* sculptor. In 1928, he made his first pieces in *pulegoso* glass, giving life to a sculptural series of vessels with impressive shapes and vivid colors, as well as an unusual collection of cacti, fruits and animals. After leaving Venini, in 1932 he founded Zecchin-Martinuzzi Vetri Artistici e Mosaici with Francesco Zecchin, for which he designed figures of animals and cacti, opaque vessels with classical shapes, and female nudes in solid *massiccio* glass. After four years, he left the company to dedicate himself exclusively to sculpture, but in the post-war period (1947) he again turned to glass. He became artistic director of Alberto Seguso's Arte Vetro where he made glass sculptures shaped while hot. Between 1953 and 1958, he designed chandeliers and glass tiles for the Vetreria Cenedese. Between the 60s and 70s, he designed works produced by Alfredo Barbini for Pauly & C.

**Benjamin Moore
(1952)**

Benjamin Moore was born in Olympia, Washington. From 1970 to 1972, he attended Central Washington University in Ellensburg, Washington. He spent 1972 at the Instituto de Artes Plasticas in Guadalajara, Mexico and in 1974, he obtained a B.F.A. with a Major in Ceramics from the California College of Arts and Crafts in Oakland. In 1977, he received an M.F.A. with a Major in Glass-Sculpture from the prestigious Rhode Island School of Design and began working as a designer for the Fostoria Glass Company in Moundsville, West Virginia. From 1978 to May of 1980, he worked at Venini in Murano where his first assignment was to help the team of *maestro* Checco Ongaro by performing various tasks. In the spring of 1979, Ongaro offered to execute some of Moore's designs. The result so impressed Ludovico Diaz de Santillana that he was asked to continue the collaboration with Venini as a designer until 1980. After several teaching positions that took him from the Niijima Glass Art Center in Tokyo to the Haystack Mountain School of Design to the Rhode Island School of Design, he presently serves as Executive Director at the Pilchuck Glass School in Stanwood, Washington. In addition, Mr. Moore owns the Artist's Glass Studio "Benjamin Moore, Inc." in Seattle, Washington.

**Yoichi Ohira
(1946)**

Yoichi Ohira was born in Japan and moved to Italy in 1973. After working as an apprentice at the Kagami Crystal Company in Tokyo, Ohira graduated in Sculpture from the Accademia di Belle Arti di Venezia with a dissertaion on the esthetics of glass. In 1973, he began working with Egidio Costantini's *Fucina degli Angeli* and participated in numerous collective and personal exhibitions presenting sculptures made with the combination of plated metal and glass. In 1987, he started a collaboration as a designer with the Vetreria de Majo in Murano. That same year, Ohira was awarded the *Premio Selezione at the Premio Murano*. He began working as an independent artist in the early 90s, creating magnificent one-of-a-kind pieces which he made in collaboration with the skillful *maestro soffiatore* (glassblower) Livio Serena and the expert *molatore* (engraver) Giacomo Barbini from Murano. He has participated in the most important international exhibitions and his works are greatly appreciated by private collectors as well as many public museums. Yoichi Ohira's work is, today, part of the permanent collections of museums such as the Victoria and Albert Museum of London, the Musée des Arts Décoratifs in Paris, the Metropolitan Museum of Art in New York, the Koganezaki Glass Museum in Shizoka, Japan and many others.

**Peter Pelzel
(1937)**

Architect and designer Peter Pelzel, the son of the engraver, Franz Pelzel, graduated in architecture in Venice in 1964. He was introduced to the world of glass during his studies (1954 ca.) when he worked for the engraving workshop S.A.L.I.R. where he created several pieces engraved by his father. His works were generally exhibited under the name of the workshop and Franz Pelzel. In the early Sixties he collaborated with Vistosi and later with La Murrina, workshops for which he created decorative glass objects and lighting. Parallel to his work as an architect, in the early 60s he designed the Lambda series for Vetrelco in Treviso.

**Alessandro Pianon
(1900-1984)**

Born in Venice, Alessandro Pianon attended the Architecture School in Venice and used his talents to become an architect and designer. He was hired by the Vetreria Vistosi in 1956 to design the company logo and ended up designing numerous collections of glass. In 1962, he started his own design studio and worked for many companies including Lumenform.

Flavio Poli
(1900-1984)

A designer, businessman, ceramic artist, Flavio Poli, was born in Chioggia. He attended the Istituto d'Arte di Venezia and began work as a designer in ceramics. In 1929, he switched to glass and designed animals, splendid *Novecento*-style nude figures in *massiccio* glass, as well as bowls and urns with figures resting on the inside, on lids or as handles for Libero Vitali's I.V.A.M. He subsequently collaborated with the Compagnia di Venezia e Murano, with the furnace of Mario and Lino Nason and with the engraver Gino Francesconi. In 1934, he accepted the artistic direction of Barovier, Seguso & Ferro, later to become Seguso Vetri d'Arte, and became a partner three years later. Together with Archimede Seguso, *maestro* of the principal team, Poli authored grandiose lighting installations, *corrosi* vessels, sculptures in *bulicante* glass, and animals in *massiccio* glass. These productions represented a milestone in the development of the glassworks of Murano. At the height of his artistic maturity, in the years between 1950 and 1960, he designed a series of *sommerso* glass pieces in a Nordic style—essential forms and sharp cold colors—which were awarded prestigious prizes including the Compasso d'Oro. He left Seguso in 1963 and between 1964 and 1966, he organized the artistic glass division at the Società Veneziana di Conterie e Cristallerie.

Giò Ponti
(1891-1979)

Gio Ponti was born in Milan. After graduating from the Architecture School in Milan, he dedicated himself to architectural design and the decorative arts, a field to which he brought significant innovation. His furniture design and his work for the porcelain manufacturer Richard Ginori, where he was an artistic consultant from 1923 to 1938, were widely acclaimed. In 1928, he founded the prestigious magazine Domus, an effective instrument for the diffusion of contemporary architectural and figurative culture. He was also one of the founders of the group Il Labirinto, which organized the first Triennali di Monza, later to become part of the Triennale di Milano. A close friend of Paolo Venini, they collaborated in experimenting with new styles and trends (forme nuove). He commissioned several lighting installations from Venini and entrusted him with the making of major stained glass windows. In 1946, he himself designed a refined collection of glass pieces for Venini: among them is the bottle with applied spiral (also made in porcelain by Richard Ginori) and the series of colored bottles and goblets a canne.

Giulio Radi
(1895-1952)

Glass technician, designer and entrepreneur, Giulio Radi was born in Murano into a family of renowned glass technicians. His first work experience was in his father's furnace, then in the furnace of Andrea Rioda. In 1921, he became one of the founders of the Successori Andrea Rioda, where his role was primarily administrative. He left the company in 1932 to become one of the founding partners of A.V.E.M. where he became artistic director in 1939. It is here that he began an intense period of design and experimentation with glass. He devoted his research in particular to the field of metal oxides where he discovered precious coloring techniques by using murrine and gold and silver dust on simple and suggestive shapes. His work was interrupted by his premature death in 1952 .

Carlo Scarpa
(1906-1978)

Born in Venice, Carlo Scarpa, graduated from the Accademia di Belle Arti in Venice in 1926. Soon after his graduation he began work at M.V.M. Cappellin where he soon replaced Vittorio Zecchin as artistic director. Following the direction laid down by Zecchin, he initially created transparent blown glass pieces with essential forms, in particular the pieces characterized by their conic base. Scarpa later designed light glass pieces in brightly colored *pasta vitrea*, or pieces decorated with festoons (*fenici*). Deservedly famous was the refined collection of *lattimi* with gold or silver leaf which he presented in Monza in 1930 together with the *canne verticali* and *millefiori* glass pieces. M.V.M. Cappellin closed for bankruptcy in 1932, putting an end to the collaboration. In 1934, Scarpa became artistic director of Venini, where he stayed through 1947. Alongside Paolo Venini, who often personally participated in the design, Carlo Scarpa experimented with the vast potential of glass, using and innovating many traditional techniques by which he created extraordinarily modern pieces. After the *mezza filigrana* glass pieces came the first *sommersi*, the *paste vitree* inspired by Chinese ceramic motifs, the *corrosi*, the *battuti*, the vessels *a fasce colorate*, *a pennellate*, the *variegati*, and the famous multicolored *murrine* with *battuto* finishes. After the war, Carlo Scarpa returned almost exclusively to his work as an architect and teacher.

Tobia Scarpa
(1935)

Son of Carlo Scarpa, Tobia Scarpa was born in Venice where he graduated from the Istituto Universitario di Architettura di Venezia. In 1958, he was invited by Paolo Venini to collaborate in the furnace, following in the footsteps of his father, Carlo, who had been with Venini during the 30s and 40s. Tobia Scarpa designed new collections for Venini even after the death of its founder, creating refined blown and glass pieces characterized by the essential quality of their design. The most successful vessels were his large *battuti*, the *Occhi* and *Murrine* series, for which he reinterpreted ancient glass techniques. As architect and designer, together with his wife Afra, he has collaborated with many companies— Cassina, B & B Italia, Flos, Molteni & C., to name a few—in creating works which belong to the best tradition of Italian design. During the 80s, he and his wife designed several glass collections for VeArt.

Archimede Seguso
(1909-1999)

Born on Murano the son of the *maestro* Antonio Seguso, Archimede Seguso began work at a very early age in the Vetreria Artistica Barovier where his father was a partner. In 1933, he was one of the founding partners of the Artistica Vetreria e Soffieria Barovier Seguso & Ferro which was later to become the Seguso Vetri d'Arte. Here, Archimede worked as *maestro* of the principal team crafting the pieces designed by Flavio Poli, and later his own pieces inspired by the *Novecento* style. He sold his share of the workshop to his partners and, in 1946, founded a new workshop, the Vetreria Artistica Archimede Seguso, where he was *primo maestro* and creator of almost all the works produced there. The first glass pieces were still inspired by the *Novecento*, as were his sculptures modeled in hot glass. At the same time, he experimented with thin blown glass textured in many ways, adapting ancient decorative techniques to the styles of the 50s such as the variations of *filigrana* which he presented throughout the decade (*Merletti, Composizione Lattimo, Piume,* etc.). During the 60s and 70s, he created intensely colored glass works such as the *colori sovrapposti* and the *fasce sovrapposte,* and further pushed the *filigrana* technique with his *Spinati,* and a *Petali* glass pieces. More recently, he based his production on strong contrasting colors. Among his latest works is the series of sculptures called *Rotture,* conceived as original works and made in solid *massiccio sommerso* glass, a realization of the profound reflections of this artist who recently died on the island of Murano.

Thomas Stearns
(1936)

Thomas Stearns was born on September 4, 1936 in Oklahoma City, U.S.A. From 1955 to 1957, he left his hometown to study painting at the Memphis Academy of Art. Between 1957 and 1959 he attended the prestigious Cranbrook Academy of Art and received a postgraduate Fulbright Travel Grant for Italy. He was 24 years old when he arrived at Venini. He started working after Christmas 1959 and stayed with the firm all of 1960 as well as 1961. He left Venice at the end of November 1962. Shortly after his departure from Venice, the Victoria & Albert Museum in London ordered a group of his works produced by Venini. In 1964, he had his first exhibition of sculpture at the Willard Gallery in New York. In 1965, he was awarded a Guggenheim Fellowship for Sculpture and a grant from the National Institute of Arts and Letters. In 1968, he had a one-man show called Constructions at the Ringling Museum of Art in Sarasota, Florida. In 1970, Thomas Stearns began teaching at The University of the Arts, Philadelphia where he was an Associate Professor in the Sculpture department. Currently retired, he resides in Philadelphia.

Lino Tagliapietra
(1934)

Lino Tagliapietra, born on Murano, was very young when he began his apprenticeship in the furnaces of Murano. In 1956, he was *maestro* at the Galliano Ferro workshop and after various collaborations with Venini and La Murrina, he went to work for Effetre International as artistic director in 1976. There he was able to perfect new glass textures which he used to make extraordinary glass pieces. Since 1979, he has taught courses in Murano glass techniques at the Pilchuck Glass School in Stanwood and in other schools in America, France, Japan and Australia, where he has come into contact and collaborated with other glass artists. Recognized as one of the most important interpreters of contemporary glass, he experiments with the material by using glass rods which he himself composes. He creates suggestive pieces that have the most magnificent colors and finishes that are often textured with special grindings. In the last few years, the artist has furthered his artistic development with a series of installations where the multiplication of single elements complete in and of themselves create a new expressive language. More recently, he has used glass to obtain large panels composed of thick rods, sectioned in different ways, which are laid down to form a brightly colored fabric with an effect comparable to extraordinary pictorial works. His works have achieved widespread acclaim and are part of the collections of major international museums such as the Victoria and Albert Museum in London, the Corning Museum of Glass in Corning, New York, the Musée des Arts Décoratifs in Paris, and others.

Ermanno Toso
(1903-1973)

Ermanno Toso was born on Murano in 1924. He began work at the Fratelli Toso workshop where he was later to become a partner. In 1936, he was named artistic and marketing director of the company. During the period preceding World War II, he created thick glass pieces using traditional decorative techniques that were characterized by simple and solid shapes inspired by the *Novecento* style. During the 50s, he created a collection of extraordinarily lightweight glass pieces based on a modern interpretation of classical techniques, such as *filigrana* and *murrina.* During the 60s, his creative talent led him towards an absolute multicolored sobriety.

Paolo Venini
(1895-1959)

Born in Milan, the entrepreneur and designer Paolo Venini was a law school graduate. From 1921 until he died, he dedicated himself to the workshop he founded, the Vetri Soffiati Muranesi Venini & C. (through 1925, Vetri Soffiati Muranesi Cappellin Venini & C.). A man of marked entrepreneurial talent, his goal from the very beginning was to expand his company's influence abroad and he sought the collaboration of the most talented artists and architects of his time, employing them as artistic directors of his company. He always worked at the side of his designers with the goal of anticipating and directing taste. He personally checked every collection produced by his furnace. And his confident esthetic choices, along with the fine quality of the products, assured his workshop both critical and commercial success. He dedicated himself personally to design from the 30s: his *Diamante* glass pieces date from 1936. Following the war, he created bottles with brightly colored *fasce* (stripes), vessels in *mosaico zanfirico* and *mosaico tessuto,* windows in *vetro mosaico* and *battuto* vessels. In collaboration with Bianconi, he created vessels such as the *fazzoletti,* which are a classic example of the production of the 50s, and were enormously successful.

Massimo Vignelli (1931)

Massimo Vignelli studied architecture in Milan and Venice. While in Venice as a student, he worked for Venini from 1953 to 1957 designing lighting fixtures, glass windows, drinking glasses, pitchers, etc. Most of the pieces he designed are today in museum collections, notably the Museum of Modern Art and the Metropolitan Museum of Art in New York, the Musée des Arts Décoratifs in Montreal, Die Neue Sammlung in Munich, and others. The work of all Venini designers throughout the years is a treasure from which one can take inspiration or learn about processes, techniques, colors, forms, textures and more. At the end is a Venini treasure from which all designers took and gave. And that is the great legacy of Paolo Venini. Based in New York, Massimo Vignelli works in the whole field of design, from graphic identity programs to publications, from products in glass, china, silver and plastic to furniture and interiors. His work has been widely recognized by museums, publications and exhibitions throughout the world.

Tapio Wirkkala (1915-1985)

Born in Finland, from 1933 to 1936 Tapio Wirkkala attended the Central School for the Industrial Arts in Helsinki where, later, he became artistic director. In 1946, he became part of the design team of the Finnish workshop, Karhula Iittala, for which he produced his most famous designs and with which he remained associated until his death. Also well known in Italy, his crystal works were shaped and cut in forms inspired by Nordic nature. A fervent scholar of materials, Wirkkala created objects not only in glass, but in metal, wood, ceramic and silver. He came to Venini for the first time in 1966 and continued his collaboration through 1972 only to return again in 1985. Wirkkala mastered Venetian techniques such as *incalmo*, *filigrana* and *murrine* with great sensitivity. The result was a series of collections of greatly refined glass pieces with extraordinary colors, which wed the purity of Nordic design to the transparency of Murano glass in an incomparable style.

Vittorio Zecchin (1878-1947)

Painter, decorator, and designer Vittorio Zecchin was the son of a glassblower from Murano. Upon graduating from the Accademia di Belle Arti di Venezia, he joined the Secessionist movement of Cà Pesaro where, on many occasions, he showed his paintings inspired by the Viennese movement. In 1913, in Munich, together with Teodoro Wolf Ferrari, he exhibited glass panels and vessels *a murrine* made by the Artisti Barovier, which represented the attempt to bring the Secessionist style to Murano glass. From 1921 to 1925, he was artistic director of the Vetri Soffiati Muranesi Cappellin Venini & C., where he created lightweight glass pieces classically inspired and delicately colored which earned him immediate success in Italy and abroad. Inspired by the styles painted in the works of 16th century painters in the Veneto, these vessels were the first modern works in Murano glass. After a short period as artistic director of the Maestri Vetrai Muranesi Cappellin & C., he collaborated with S.A.L.I.R. in the 30s, providing drawings for glass engraving and personally decorating glass with enamels. He occasionally worked for Ferro Toso (1930), A.V.E.M. (1932), Seguso Vetri d'Arte (1933-34). At Fratelli Toso (1938), he created the elegant *leggerissimi* (lightweight) goblets. During the 20s and 30s, Zecchin also designed tapestries, mosaics, embroidery, ceramics, furniture, silverware—all of which he exhibited at the Biennali di Venezia and Monza. During the last years of his life, he dedicated himself to teaching.

Mary Ann "Toots" Zynsky (1951)

Designer Mary Ann "Toots" Zynsky was born in Boston and attended the Rhode Island School of Design, the Pilchuck Glass School and the Craft School at Haystack, taking part in various experiences and experiments. From 1981 to 1983, she collaborated with Venini, where, with the help of *maestro* Checco Ongaro, she created a remarkable series of pieces. Among these are the vessels titled *Chiacchere* and *Folto* whose openings have wide turned-over lips and decorations with glass rods produced out of hair-thin threads made with a technique she invented herself. Her works are present not only in the major international museums, but also in the White House amidst the works of the best American artists.

Vetrerie (Workshops)

A.VE. M.
(Arte Vetraria Muranese)

A.V.E.M. was founded in 1932 by Antonio Luigi Ferro, his son Egidio and the *maestri* glassblowers Emilio Nason, Galliano Ferro and Giulio Radi. During the 30s the furnace, which was capable, of producing refined Venetian glass techniques, worked with Vittorio Zecchin who created lightweight blown glass pieces, and Emilio Nason who created *Novecento* styled sculptures. After 1939, Giulio Radi became artistic director and dedicated himself predominantly to experimenting with metal oxides. After Radi's premature death in 1952, Giorgio Ferro replaced him and acted as artistic director through 1955, the year he left to found a new furnace with his father, Galliano. During the 50s, A.V.E.M. collaborated with the painter Luigi Scarpa Croce, and later the designer Anzolo Fuga. Between 1966 and 1972 several collections were designed by the glassmaster Luciano Ferro. A.V.E.M. is still active in Murano today.

Vetreria Alfredo Barbini

Alfredo Barbini worked as an apprenticeship at S.A.I.A.R. Ferro Toso and the Società Anonima Vetrerie e Cristallerie di Murano. He also worked as a glassblower in furnaces such as Barovier Seguso & Ferro, V.A.M.S.A., and in particular, Gino Cenedese & C., where he served as the artistic director. In 1950, Alfredo Barbini opened his own furnace. Skilled in the hot-work manipulation of *massiccio* glass, Barbini channeled his development toward researching the malleability of glass, his preference for essential forms increasing more and more. After the 60s, Flavio Barbini joined his father in both the administration of the company and product design. Today, the company is still one of the most important glassmakers of Murano.

Artisti Barovier - Vetreria Artistica Barovier - Ferro Toso Barovier - Barovier Toso & C. Barovier & Toso

Giovanni Barovier and his nephews Giuseppe, Benvenuto and Benedetto, worked as glassblowers at the Salviati dott. Antonio furnace founded in 1877. In 1884, after Salviati's departure, they acquired ownership of the company. On the basis of an agreement signed with Salviati, the company maintained its original name until Salviati's death in 1890. It then changed its name to Artisti Barovier. Under the guidance of Benvenuto and Giuseppe, the company reproduced the classical themes of 19th century glass and soon achieved fame for the refined in its production. Later developed works, particularly *a murrine*, were inspired by floral themes. The Artisti Barovier took several of these pieces to different exhibitions, including the Cà Pesaro (1908, 1909, 1913) where pieces designed by Zecchin and Wolf-Ferrari were also shown. During World War I, the furnace was temporarily moved to Livorno in Tuscany. In 1919, the company name was changed to Vetreria Artistica Barovier and several new partners were added. Among them were Ercole Barovier, Nicolò Barovier, Benvenuto Barovier's sons and Giuseppe Barovier's son, Napoleone. In 1926, Ercole and Nicolò Barovier took over the management of the company and both became artistic directors, creating, among other things, sophisticated multicolored vessels *a murrine* and singular animals in blown glass.
After 1932, Nicolò and Ercole Barovier became sole proprietors of the company. Ercole Barovier designed many objects which earned the company remarkable success, among them the *Primavera* series. A tireless creator of new collections and glass textures, Ercole Barovier dedicated himself to perfecting the *colorazione a caldo senza fusione* which he began using during the second half of the 30s. In 1936, after the separation from his brother Nicolò, Ercole Barovier became partner of the S.A.I.A.R. Ferro Toso, forming Ferro Toso e Barovier. In 1939, it became Barovier Toso & C. And finally, in 1942, its name became Barovier & Toso. Ercole Barovier remained artistic director of the company through 1972 and was succeeded by his son, Angelo, who was already a designer for the company. During 80s and until today, many designers collaborated with Barovier & Toso. Among them are Matteo Thun, Toni Zuccheri, Renato and Giusto Toso, and Noti Massari. The most recent production of the company, now directed by Angelo, his son Jacopo and Giovanni Toso, has been created largely by designers such as Roberto Caddeo, Marco Mencacci, Franco Raggi, Luca Scacchetti and others.

Cappellin Venini & C.
Vetri Soffiati Muranesi

Cappellin Venini & C. was founded in 1921 from the meeting among the Venetians Giacomo Cappellin and Luigi Ceresa, the Milan-born Paolo Venini and the German-born Emilio Ochs. It first settled in the furnace abandoned by Andrea Rioda. Rioda had died prematurely leaving the technical direction of his company to Giovanni Seguso, better known to some as "Patare". Under the artistic direction of Vittorio Zecchin, Cappellin Venini & C. produced collections characterized by essential forms, some of which were inspired by the Renaissance glass pieces reproduced by 16th century painters in the Veneto region. The company received widespread acclaim at the major exhibitions of decorative arts of the 20s such as the Biennale di Monza (1923,1925), the Biennale di Venezia (1924), and the Paris Exposition (1925). Cappellin and Venini separated due to irreconcilable differences and the company was closed in May 1925. Subsequently Paolo Venini and Ochs took the furnace and created a new company named Vetri Soffiati Muranesi Venini & C. Giacomo Cappellin took the glassblowers and Vittorio Zecchin with him and founded a new company with a new furnace; the Maestri Vetrai Muranesi Cappellin & C.

Maestri Vetrai Muranesi Cappellin & C.

M.V.M. Cappellin & C. was founded in 1925 by Giacomo Cappellin after the closing of Cappellin Venini & C. Vittorio Zecchin, a painter from Murano who had worked for Cappellin Venini, continued his collaboration with Cappellin for a short time designing *soffiati*, blown glass pieces characterized by delicate colors and pure lines. At the end of 1926, following Zecchin's departure, the young Carlo Scarpa took over the artistic direction of the company. Initially, he proceeded along the course taken by his predecessor, creating lightweight blown pieces with simple geometric forms. These were followed by many collections of refined elegance characterized by various transparent textures often distinguished by vivid colors. Despite the remarkable success at the 1930 Biennale di Monza, M.V.M. Cappellin & C. was forced to close in January 1932. Most probably, this was a result of inefficient financial management.

Vetreria Archimede Seguso

Vetreria Archimede Seguso was founded in 1946 by Archimede Seguso, partner and *maestro* at Seguso Vetri d'Arte until 1942. Seguso was not only the tireless creator of almost all the collections produced by Vetreria Archimede Seguso, he executed his own works and experimented with new techniques and materials. He participated in the Biennali di Venezia and the Triennali di Milano from 1950 on, presenting among other things, his personal interpretations of the ancient technique of *filigrana*. His interpretaions, vessels often enriched with applications of gold leaf, he called *Merletti*. The company is now run by his son Gino Seguso, with the assistance of his grandson Antonio Seguso.

Seguso Vetri d'Arte

In 1933, several *maestri* who had left Vetreria Artistica Barovier, together with Archimede, Ernesto and Alberto Seguso, founded the Vetreria e Soffieria Barovier Seguso & Ferro. Muranese painter Vittorio Zecchin took on the art direction for a short time with Flavio Poli replacing him in 1934. The company was reorganized in 1937 to become Seguso Vetri d'Arte. At this time, Poli also became a partner and with the assistance of the *maestro* Archimede Seguso, they created animals and sculptures in thick glass which were widely acclaimed at the Biennali of that period. After a new company re-organization in the 50s and 60s, the workshop produced a remarkable series of *sommersi* pieces, as well as the *Valve* and the unique *Siderali* pieces. The latter were designed by Flavio Poli, who remained in the company until 1963. After he left, Mario Pinzoni took over the artistic direction and remained stylistically faithful to his predecessor. Since the early 60s, the company has been directed by Maurizio Albarelli.

Aureliano Toso Vetri Decorativi

Founded in 1938 by Aureliano Toso, Aureliano Toso Vetri Decorativi boasted the artistic direction of Dino Martens, a painter from Murano, who worked with the company until 1965. The works created by Dino Martens brought widespread acclaim at the major exhibitions of decorative arts, the colors being of particular interest. In 1962, the company sought the collaboration of outside consultants such as Enrico Potz. After 1966, the artistic direction was entrusted to Gino Poli, who designed, among others, the collection *A Solchi Colorati*. Later the company turned to the production of glass parts for lighting, which it still produces today.

Fratelli Toso

Founded in 1854 by the brothers Ferdinando, Carlo, Liberato, Angelo, Giovanni and Gregorio Toso, Fratelli Toso initially produced pharmaceutical bottles for domestic use. These were soon followed by reproductions of antique glass pieces. In the early 1900s, the company produced objects and chandeliers in *Liberty* style executed with the *murrine* technique. In 1912 and 1914, Fratelli Toso obtained great success at the Biennale di Venezia by presenting works by the Norwegian artist Hans Stoltberg Lerche. During the 20s, the company produced traditional *soffiati*, however, in 1934 a remarkable change, in their work was noticed at the Biennale di Venezia. In 1936, the artistic direction of the company was taken by Ermanno Toso, who progressively revisited the techniques of Murano glass reinterpreting them in a personal style which obtained widespread consensus—especially after World War II. During the 60s and 70s, the works of Renato, Giusto and Rosanna Toso, who often used transparent glass, brought a decidedly modern look to the company. The furnace was closed in 1982.

Vetri Soffiati Muranesi Venini & C. Venini & C. - Venini S.p.a.

In 1925, following the closing of Cappellin Venini & C., Paolo Venini founded his own glass company, which he called Vetri Soffiati Muranesi Venini & C. While the company, under the artistic direction of sculptor Napoleone Martinuzzi, produced collections designed by Vittorio Zecchin, it soon became known for the *pulegosi*, an original style created by Venini and Martinuzzi. In 1932, both Martinuzzi and Zecchin left the company. Paolo Venini changed the name of the company in to Venini & C. and the Milanese architect Tomaso Buzzi became the new artistic director. After 1934, artistic direction was taken on by Carlo Scarpa who designed most of the company's production through 1947.
Side by side with Venini, who often intervened personally in design, Scarpa created numerous collections of objects characterized by refined colors. After World War II, Venini & C. sought numerous collaborations with artists such as architect Giò Ponti, Swedish born Tyra Lundgren. After 1948, Fulvio Bianconi, Massimo Vignelli and Tobia Scarpa contributed significantly to the new direction of the company. Paolo Venini died in 1959 and his son-in-law, Ludovico Diaz de Santillana took over the management of Venini & C.
He not only worked personally as a glass designer but also continued the collaboration started by Paolo Venini with various artists and designers. Starting in 1960 many other designers collaborated with the company; among them Thomas Stearns, Toni Zuccheri, Tapio Wirkkala, Laura Diaz de Santillana and Alessandro Diaz de Santillana, James Carpenter, Dan Dailey, Richard Marquis, Benjamin Moore and Toots Zynsky. In 1986, the Diaz de Santillana family left the company selling their stock to the Ferruzzi group, which guaranteed the fine quality Venini was known for by hiring new designers such as Timo Sarpaneva, Marco Zanini, Ettore Sottsass Jr., Alessandro Mendini, Mario Bellini, Barbara del Vicario and others. Since 1988, the company, now called Venini S.p.a. and lead by Dott. Luigi Lucchetta, has been part of the financial group Royal Scandinavian.

Vetreria Vistosi

The descendant of an ancient dynasty of Murano glassmakers, Guglielmo Vistosi opened the Vistosi furnace in 1945 to produce glass components for lighting. After his death in 1952, the direction of the company was taken over by his brother, Oreste, and his nephews Gino and Luciano. They carried on the line of production serving as designers as well. Vistosi also sought the collaboration of many independent artists and designers such as Alessandro Pianon, Peter Pelzel and Fulvio Bianconi. During the 60s, the company, successful for its essential forms and the sobriety of its colors, received many awards. During the following decade, its production was designed by Angelo Mangiarotti, Enrico Capuzzo, Gae Aulenti, Vico Magistretti, Elenore Peduzzi Riva and Ettore Sottsass Jr. After the company's change of ownership, the furnace produced glass components for lighting until it was closed in the early 90s.

Zecchin-Martinuzzi Vetri Artistici e Mosaici

In 1932, the two Muranese partners of Paolo Venini, engineer Francesco Zecchin and the sculptor and designer Napoleone Martinuzzi, left the Vetri Soffiati Muranesi Venini & C. and founded their own company, Zecchin-Martinuzzi Vetri Artistici e Mosaici. Its production was directed by Napoleone Martinuzzi who, inspired by the sculptural qualities of the *Novecento* movement, created large vessels in opaque glass, animals and *cactus* in *pasta vitrea* and female nudes in *massiccio* glass. In some cases the company also collaborated with Mario Romano and Giovanni Guerrini. Napoleone Martinuzzi left the company in 1936, and after two years Francesco Zecchin closed it for good.

Glossary

Types of glass

Avventurina
Glass with a distinctive bright metallic look created by adding small particles of copper to the molten glass. The word *avventurina* originated to describe the difficulty of its production, considered to be a *ventura* (an adventure in Venetian dialect). It is produced by gradually adding to the *cristallo* glass mixture the required quantities of reducing substances. After a very slow cooling process the reduced glass mixture will produce small copper crystals. The copper crystals, when separated from the melted mixture, will give the glass an unusual copper finish. (See illustration n. 6)

Colorazione a caldo senza fusione
Obtained from a basic mixture similar to the *cristallo* glass, it owes its distinctive irregular coloring to the addition into the molten glass of substances that do not melt or do not have time to melt. This technique is credited to the research conducted by Ercole Barovier, who used it frequently. (See illustration n. 121)

Cristallo
In artistic glasswork this is the name for clear glass whose quality depends mainly on the purity of the raw materials used to make it. *Cristallo* must contain the least possible quantity of coloring oxides. To remove the oxides, de-coloring substances can be used during the melting process to neutralize their effect. Murano *cristallo* is distinguished from lead crystal and Bohemian crystal by a longer cooling time, which allows more working time for the molten glass. This is caused by the significant presence of soda and calcium oxides in the molten glass mixture. (See illustration n. 49)

Lattimo
White glass made to resemble porcelain. The unique opaqueness and milk-white color is created by adding significant quantities of small crystals of calcium and soda fluorides to the molten glass. The degree of refraction is different from basic molten glass. This is due to the crystallization that occurs when the zinc oxide and the fluoride-based compounds separate during the cooling phase. (See illustration n. 45)

Pasta vitrea
Opaque colored glass whose consistency is made to appear like ceramic, *pasta vitrea* is obtained by adding considerable quantities of white opalescent, clear or colored crystals to the molten glass. It is difficult to control because the long cooling time of the *pasta vitrea* can sometimes change the final appearance of the object. This is why *pasta vitrea* is more often used for trimmings or applied decorations than for a whole vessel. (See illustrations nn. 21 and 22)

Primavera
The *Primavera* series, designed by Ercole Barovier and made by the Vetreria Artistica Barovier & C. in the early 30s, is distinguished by a milky white *craquelé* glass with the addition of black or blue *pasta vitrea* trim and decoration. There was a very limited production of this series due to the fact that it was a result of a glass mixture obtained accidentally so it could never be replicated. (See illustration n. 7)

Pulegoso
Translucent glass that is identified by a countless number of burst and unburst bubbles— *puleghe* in the dialect of Murano—contained in the glass. These bubbles are created by adding substances such as petroleum to the molten glass. The bubbles are then released during the heating process. (See illustrations nn. 13 and 14)

Soffiati
Blown glass pieces characterized by delicate colors and pure lines. (See illustrations nn. 8 and 10)

Trasparente colorato
Composed of a basic mixture similar to *cristallo* glass. Based on various known chemical formulas, the color is achieved by adding metallic oxides to the molten glass. The color will depend on the type of reactions the metallic oxides produce. (See illustration n. 9)

Techniques

Filigrana
A technique dating back to the 16th century used to manufacture glass objects composed of clear glass rods with a core of *lattimo* or colored glass filament. The rods are laid side by side, placed in the kiln and fused together. They are then gathered at the end of the blow pipe on a cylinder of *cristallo* glass, which is then blown and shaped. This technique utilizes three different patterns: *mezza-filigrana*, *a reticello* and *a retortoli* (*zanfirico*). In the *a mezza-filigrana* and *a reticello* patterns, rods with a single filament are used. (See illustrations nn. 43 and 44). A *retortoli* or *zanfirico* pattern is composed of at least two filaments woven into a spiral. A *reticello* is a pattern of diamond shaped filaments obtained by merging, while twisting in the opposite directions, two half spheres of *mezza filigrana*. A more ancient variation of *filigrana* is the *a retortoli*, also known as *zanfirico*. This variation is named after the Venetian antiquarian Antonio Sanquirico who, during the first half of the 19th century, commissioned a large quantity of glass made using this particular technique. During the 50s and 60s *maestro* Archimede Seguso further developed the *filigrana* technique by inventing new interpretations called *merletti* (see illustrations nn. 114 and 115) using segments of specially prepared *a retortoli* rods.

Incalmo
The *incalmo* technique consists of joining different pieces of glass while hot, then shaping them into the desired form. If repeated, this process can create objects composed of several colored sections. (See illustrations nn. 141 and 145)

Incamiciato
Glass composed of one or more cased layers. Generally colored transparent glass, or sometimes *pasta vitrea*, is laid over a base of opaque glass. This technique, which allows for sophisticated color effects, has been widely used since the 20s and continues to be widely used today. (See illustrations nn. 80 and 81)

Massiccio
A process by which objects and sculptures of thick glass are made. Widely used in Murano since the beginning of the 30s, it consists of shaping the glass while still malleable with the help of tools and/or molds but without blowing. (See illustration n. 133)

Mosaico or A Murrine
First introduced in Roman times and reintroduced at the end of the 19th century by the Muranese glass industry, this process is based on joining sections of glass rods called *murrine*. The glass sections are obtained by cutting multicolored rods of glass. These rods were often produced in advance to specification, sometimes by different glass workshops, to create a floral or geometric design. The *murrine* are laid down in the desired pattern, fused together into a single glass mass and then blown and shaped by the glassblower. (See illustrations nn. 1, 2, 3, 4 and 4). In some cases, as with Carlo Scarpa in the 40s, molds are used and the glass is shaped without blowing. (See illustrations nn. 65, 66 and 67) Carlo Scarpa also used two distinctive finishing processes: *inciso*, *battuto* and *velato*. (See illustrations nn. 61, 62, 63 and 64). These finishings were obtained by carving at the wheel the entire surface in the *moleria*.

Sommerso
Glass of significant weight and thickness composed of clear and colored *cristallo*, which is obtained by repeatedly dipping the object during the work process into different crucibles of melted glass. (See illustration n. 112) There are many variations to this technique. In fact, some layers of clear glass may be substituted with other types of glass, such as glass with bubbles (called *sommerso a bollicine*) with gold or silver leaf. (See illustrations nn. 41 and 42). These inclusions create beautiful multicolored or multilayered effects.

Tessere
Glass composed of patches of various sizes and shapes. The *tessere* are obtained either by flattening segments of glass rods (see illustrations nn. 128 and 130) or by subdividing sheets of colored glass into the desired shapes (see illustrations nn. 86 and 87). After placing them in the desired pattern on a heat-resistant flat surface, they are then fused together, blown and shaped.

Tessuto
A multicolored glass obtained by the juxtaposition of thin vertical rods fused together. After fusing the rods, which are generally laid down in alternating colors, the *maestro* gathers them into a cylinder which is then blown and shaped. In some cases the object may be finished with a fine grinding (*velato*) at the wheel. (See illustrations nn. 52, 53, 54, 146 and 147)

Hot decorative techniques

Applicazioni a caldo
This name refers to objects decorated with applications of glass. Adhered during the hot working process onto the surface of the object (see illustrations nn. 32 and 33), these applications may be in relief, as in the case of *bugne* (see illustration n. 46) or encased within the wall during a successive phase of the work process, as in the case of *a fili* (see illustrations nn. 69 and 75), *a fasce* (see illustration n. 68) or *pennellate*. (See illustrations nn. 72, 73 and 74)

Applicazione di foglia d'oro o d'argento
Done during the work process, this type of decoration is executed by applying very fine leaves of gold or silver around the wall of the object. Once the leaves are applied the piece is blown and a fragmentation of the leaf occurs. Sometimes the pieces are encased with a thin layer of *cristallo* glass.
(See illustrations nn. 28, 29 and 30)

Fenicio
Decoration achieved by the application of stripes or threads of colored *pasta vitrea* which are then combed with a special tool to obtain a festoon-like pattern. It owes its name to the decorations found on several Phoenician and Egyptian glass works. It may be on the surface in relief or encased within.
(See illustrations nn. 23, 24 and 25)

Millefiori
Lattimo glass decorated with *murrine millefiori* encased in the glass during the work process. Once the *murrine* have been gathered on the surface of the glass, they are cased with a thin layer of clear or lightly colored glass. (See illustration n. 26)

Iridato
Glass with an iridescent look achieved by exposing the object during the annealing process to the vapors of tin, titanium or other metals. The heat radiated by the hot piece creates a thin layer of metallic oxide on the surface of the glass, which will then reflect light in an irregular manner.
(See illustration n. 27)

Cold decorative techniques

Corroso
This rough surface decoration is obtained by the corrosive action of hydrofluoric acid. Usually this decoration is founded in thick-walled glass objects. The object is first powdered in sawdust and then soaked in acid, which creates the irregular *corroso* surface.
(See illustrations nn. 46 and 47)

Inciso - Battuto - Velato
These cold decorative techniques are all executed with the use of a grinding wheel in the *moleria*.
An *inciso* decor generally consists of vertical thin incisions executed on the surface of the glass.
(See illustrations nn. 60 and 61)
A decoration of deeper and wider wheel carving used on metal to imitate the *martelé* is called *battuto*.
(See illustrations nn. 62 and 64)
When the same wheel carving is applied in a lighter and softer way to give the glass a satin finish it is called *velato*. (See illustration n. 63)

Bibliography

1921
- G. Lorenzetti, *I vetri di Murano*, Le vie d'Italia, October.

1922
- F. Sapori, The 13th *Esposizione d'Arte a Venezia*, Bergamo.
- R. Linzeler, *Les verreries de Cappellin Venini*, Art et Decoration.

1923
- C. Carrà, *L'arte decorativa contemporanea*, Milan.
- R. Linzeler, *I vetri soffiati muranesi di Cappellin e Venini*, Arte pura e decorativa.
- R. Papini, *Le Arti a Monza 1923*, Bergamo.
- R. Papini, *La mostra delle Arti decorative a Monza*, Emporium, July.

1926
- U. Nebbia, La 15th *Esposizione d'Arte a Venezia*, Bergamo.
- *I vetri di Murano e i vetri soffiati Venini & C.*, Le tre Venezie, May.
- H. Clouzot, *Les arts appliqués, in La Renaissance de l'art francaise et des l'industries de luxe*, November.
- V. Costantini, *Maestri vetrai muranesi Cappellin*, Le Arti Plastiche, July 16.
- P. Du Colombier, *Le Salon d'Automne*, Art et Decoration, November.
- Salon d'Automne, *Catalogue des Ouvrages de peinture, sculpture, dessin, architecture et art décoratif*, Paris, Puyfourcat.

1927
- *Artisti italiani a Ginevra*, Le Arti Plastiche, February.
- 13rd *Mostra Internazionale delle Arti Decorative*, Exhibition catalogue Milano, Ceschina.
- *Cose veneziane*, Le Arti Plastiche, August 16.
- G. Dell'Oro, *I veneti alla III Biennale delle Arti Decorative di Monza*, Le Tre Venezie, August.
- *Exposition d'artistes italiens contemporaines*, Exhibition catalogue, Torino, Stab. grafico Foa.
- R. G., *Il Padiglione di Venezia alla I Fiera di Tripoli*, Rivista di Venezia, February.
- *XCIII Esposizione di Belle Arti della Società Amatori e Cultori di Belle Arti*, Catalogue, Rome, Pinci. *20 Espositori a Monza*, Le Arti Plastiche, September 16. 2nd *Mostra d'arte marinara e I mostra d'arte fiumana*, Catalogue, Roma, Pinci.
- *Le mostre di Ginevra*, Le Arti Plastiche, March 1st.
- G. Marangoni, *Arti del fuoco. Ceramica, vetri, vetrate. Enciclopedia delle moderne Arti decorative*, Milano, Ceschina.
- G. Marangoni, *La terza mostra internazionale delle arti decorative nella Villa Reale di Monza. Notizie, rilievi, risultati*, Bergamo, Istituto di Arti Grafiche.
- R. Papini, *Le Arti a Monza nel 1927: gli italiani*, Emporium, n. 391.
- F. Reggiori, *La terza Biennale delle arti decorative a Monza*, Architettura e arti decorative, 1927-1928, pamphlet n. 7.
- Salon d'Automne, *Catalogue des Ouvrages de peinture, sculpture, dessin, architecture et art décoratif*, Paris, Puyfourcat.

- E. Zorzi, *Cronache d'arte. Mostre in preparazione. Una mostra d'arte italiana a Ginevra*. Le Tre Venezia, February.
- E. Zorzi, *I vetrai italiani a Lipsia*, Le Tre Venezie, March.

1928
- C.A. Felice, *Le Arti decorative. Vetri di Orrefors e di Murano. Argenti di Fegarotti. La Scuola d' Arte di Padova*, Domus, July.
- *Bollettino delle istituzioni. La famiglia artistica*, Le Arti Plastiche, March 1st.
- G. Dell'Oro, *Le piccole industrie venete all'esposizione di Torino*, Le Tre Venezie, July.
- *Filigrane di Murano. Un'arte che riappare in forme nuove*, Domus, January.
- A. Lancelotti, *La terza mostra internazionale delle arti decorative a Monza*, Almanacco Italiano, vol. 33.
- A. Marzocchi, *Ambienti milanesi, la famiglia artistica*, La Casa Bella, December.
- *Murano: oggi fatto d'arte*, Domus, December.
- A. Parini, *La Mostra piemontese dell'artigianato*, La Casa Bella, November.
- *Salon d'Automne. Catalogue des Ouvrages de peinture, sculpture, dessin, architecture et art décoratif*, Paris, Puyfourcat.

1929
- *Nuovi Vetri Muranesi*, Domus, February.
- M. Croci, *Gli italiani al Salon d'Automne*, La Casa Bella, December.
- M. Dazzi, *Le industrie venete alla X Fiera Campionaria di Milano*, Le Tre Venezie, May.
- *L'Italie à la Foire de Paris*, Paris, Gargagnoni.
- Exhibition catalogue, *Artisti italiani contemporanei*, Galleria Pesaro.
- Catalogue, *Milano Bestetti e Tuminelli*.
- *Nuovi vetri di Giacomo Cappellin*, Domus, April.
- *Nuovi vetri di Giacomo Cappellin*, Domus, October.
- R.S. *Le ultime settimane della mostra di Barcellona*, L'illustrazione italiana, December.

1930
- A. Cassi Ramelli, *L'illuminazione alla Triennale di Monza*, L'illuminazione razionale.
- *Acquisti a Monza*, Le Arti Plastiche, November 1st.
- C.A. Felice, Catalogue of the 4th *Esposizione internazionale delle Arti Decorative ed industriali Moderne*, Milan, Ceschina.
- C.A. Felice, *I vetri alla Triennale di Monza*, Dedalo, pamphlet n. 5.
- *Alla Triennale di Monza*, Domus, July.
- *Alla Triennale di Monza, Cappellin nella galleria dei vetri d'arte*, Domus, September.
- *Guida all'arredamento*, La Casa Bella, August.
- *I premiati alla Esposizione Internazionale di Barcellona alla Mostra di Belle Arti*, La Casa Bella, February.
- *La Biennale di Monza*, Le Arti Plastiche, April 1st.

- *Monza II*, Le Arti Plastiche, July 16th.
- U. Nebbia, *I veneti alle arti decorative di Monza*, Le Tre Venezie, June.
- *Nuovi vetri di Giacomo Cappellin*, Domus, January.
- R. Pacini, *La IV Triennale d'arti decorative a Monza. Il - Le sezioni italiane*, Emporium, n. 431.
- *Premi a Monza*, Le Arti Plastiche, October 16th.
- G. Ponti, *La Triennale alla Villa Reale di Monza*, Le Arti Plastiche, October.
- U. Nebbia, *XVII Esposizione Internazionale d'Arte*, Venice.
- R. Papini, *le Arti d'Oggi*, Milan-Rome.
- F. Reggiori, *La Triennale di Monza, IV Mostra Internazionale delle Arti Decorative, in Architettura e arti decorative*, pamphlet n. 11.
- R. Targetti, *La partecipazione italiana all'Esposizione Internazionale di Barcellona a cura del Commissario generale del governo*, Milan.

1931
- G. Lorenzetti, *Vetri di Murano*, Bergamo.
- C.A. Felice, *Siamo nella storia*, Domus, January.
- Catalogue of the *20th Esposizione dell'Opera Bevilacqua La Masa*, Venice, stamp. Zanetti.
- G. Dell'Oro, *Le arti decorative alla Mostra di Cà Pesaro*, Le Tre Venezie, August.
- Erredi, *Vetri, ceramiche e merletti alla mostra di Amsterdam*, Le Tre Venezie, March.
- C.A. Felice, *Richiamo alle arti decorative*, Domus, October.
- F. Geraci, *I veneti alla I Quadriennale Romana d'Arte*, Le Tre Venezie, February.
- Gida, *Giardini veneti e veneziani alla mostra di Palazzo Vecchio*, Rivista di Venezia, June.
- *I Quadriennale d'arte nazionale*, Catalogue, Rome, Pinci.
- *La Mostra d'arte veneziana al Museo di Amsterdam*, Rivista di Venezia, April.
- *La pagina illustrata dell'industria artigiana*, Le Tre Venezie, February.
- *Mostra del Giardino Italiano*, Catalogue, Florence, Ariani.
- *Mostra di vetri, ceramiche e merletti d'arte moderna italiana*, Catalogue.
- *Mostre Veneziane*, Le Arti Plastiche, August 16th.
- U. Nebbia, *Una mostra d'arte decorativa italiana ad Amsterdam*, Emporium, n. 439.
- *Nuova arte decorativa veneziana a Cà Pesaro*, Domus, July.
- *Settimana italiana in Atene*, Catalogue, Rome, Squarci.

1932
- P. Chiesa, *Il vetro alla Biennale veneziana*, Domus, July.
- P. Chiesa, *Vetri incisi a Venezia*, Domus, August.
- U. Nebbia, *L'Arte decorativa alla Biennale*, Le Tre Venezie, May.
- V. Querel, *Modernità e sintesi nel vetro di Murano*, Rassegna dell'istruzione artistica, July.
- G. Lorenzetti, *Il museo vetrario di Murano*, Le Tre Venezie, September.

1933
- *Aspetti di una nuova dimora in Firenze*, Domus, October.
- *Bianco e nero. Specchio e cristallo*, Domus, November.

1934
- Catalogue of the *19th Biennale, 1934*, Ferrari, Venezia.
- *Suggerimenti*, Domus, September.
- *I tipi nei vetri d'arte a Venezia*, Domus, November.
- *La tavola e i regali di Natale*, Domus, December.
- E. Motta, *Guida della XIX Biennale*.
- E. Motta, *L'Arte decorativa*, Le Tre Venezie, May.
- R. Papini, *Vetri di Paolo Venini*, Le Tre Venezie, May.

1935
- G. Dell'Oro, *Punte d'arte decorativa veneziana in Polonia*, Le Tre Venezie, January.

1936
- Catalogue of the 20th *Biennale di Venezia 1936*, Ferrari, Venice.
- Catalogue of the *Triennale*, Milano, S.A.M.E.
- E.N.A.P.I. *L'artigianato d'Italia alla VI Triennale di Milano*, Milan.
- G. Dell'Oro, *L'arte decorativa alla XX Biennale*, Le Tre Venezie, July.
- G. Dell'Oro, *Ambienti, mobili e arredi veneti alla VI Triennale di Milano*, Le Tre Venezie, August-September.
- C.A. Felice, *Arti industriali oggi*, Quaderni della Triennale, Milan, Ceschina.
- G. Ponti, *Considerazioni sui vetri Venini*, Domus, July.
- *Utili regali per Natale che vi consigliamo*, Domus, December.
- Venini Murano, *advertisement*, Le Tre Venezie, July.
- Venini Murano, *advertisements*, Le Tre Venezie, August-September.
- G. Ponti, *La battaglia di Parigi*, Domus, October.

1937
- *In visita alle case*, Domus, February.

1938
- G. Dell'Oro, *L'Arte decorativa alla 21st Biennale*, Le Tre Venezie, May.
- Illustrated pages of the *Istituto Veneto per il Lavoro*, Le Tre Venezie, May.
- Catalogue of the *21st Biennale 1938*, Ferrari, Venice.
- *Una piccola collezione di bomboniere da nozze*, Domus, May.
- *Regali per la signora, Regali per una giovane*, Domus, December.
- Vetri di Venini, *advertisements*, Le Tre Venezie, June.

1939
- *Ardimenti in una casa*, Domus, February.
- *Gli interni di una nuova casa*, Domus, May.

248

1940
- Catalogue of the *22nd Biennale 1940*, Ferrari, Venice.
- G. Dell'Oro, *Artigiani e produttori veneti alla VII Triennale*, Le Tre Venezie, May.
- R. Papini, Emporium.
- G. Ponti, *Venini o della castigatezza*, Domus, June.
- G. Ponti, *Nuovi vetri muranesi*, Domus, October.
- E. Motta, *Vetri e merletti*, Le Tre Venezie, July-August.
- *Barovier-Toso alla Triennale*, Domus, May.

1941
- C.A. Felice, *Contro la produzione fittizia*, Domus, January.
- *Mobili in vetro*, Lo Stile.
- *Vetrina di Venini*, Lo Stile.
- C.A. Felice, *La produzione vetraria italiana*, Lo Stile.
- *Possibilità del vetro moderno*, Domus, February.

1942
- G. Dell'Oro, *La XXIII Biennale Veneziana, 3rd Rassegna dell'Arte decorativa*, Tre Venezie, September-October.

1943
- C.E. Rava, *Funzionale antico e nuovo*, Domus, March.
- G. Dell'Oro, *Il rinnovamento della produzione del vetro muranese*, Le Tre Venezie, November-December.

1944
- *Venini*, Art et décoration, November.

1945
- R. Aloi, *L'arredamento moderno*, 3rd series, Milan, Hoepli.

1950
- *Arte decorativa alla XXV Biennale*, Domus, October.

1951
- 9th *Triennale di Milano*, Exhibition catalogue, Milan.
- *I vetri italiani alla Triennale*, Domus, October.
- *L'Art du verre*, Exhibition catalogue, Paris.

1952
- R. Aloi, *L'arredamento moderno*, Milan.
- *Munari e la qualità italiana*, Domus, August.
- *26th Biennale*, Catalogue, Ferrari, Venice.
- G. Mariacher, *Mostra storica del vetro muranese*, Catalogue of the 26th Biennale of Venice.
- *Murano alla Biennale*, Domus, November.

1953
- *Regali di Natale*, Domus, December.

1954
- G. Mariacher, *L'arte del vetro*, Milan, Mondadori.
- *Arti decorative alla Biennale*, Domus, October.
- *Trent'anni di Triennale*, Domus, November.
- *Il nuovo negozio Olivetti a New York*, Domus, September.

1955
- R. Aloi, *Esempi di decorazione moderna di tutto il mondo; Vetri d'oggi*, Milan, Hoepli.
- *Piccola rassegna di Venini*, Domus, April.
- *Le nuove lampade di Venini con Massimo Vignelli*, Domus, December.

1956
- *Verres Murano*, Catalogue of the exhibition at the Museum of Decorative Arts, Paris.
- *Venini vasi, Venini lampade*, Domus, January.
- *Arti decorative a Venezia*, Domus, November.

1957
- *Venini in Europa*, Domus, July.

1958
- A. Gasparetto, *Il vetro di Murano dalle origini ad oggi*, Venice.
- G. Mariacher, *Venedig zeigt Glas aus Murano*, Venice.

1959
- G. Ponti, *Venini*, Domus, December.

1960
- A. Gasparetto, *Vetri di Murano 1860-1960*, Exhibition catalogue, Verona.

1962
- *Nuovi vetri Venini*, Domus, January.

1963
- A. Gasparetto, *Mostra del vetro di Murano*, Exhibition catalogue, Venice.
- *Venini 1963, Vetro e argento*, Domus, July.

1964
- *32nd Biennale Internazionale d'Arte*, Catalogue, Stamperia di Venezia, Venice.

1965
- G. Perocco, *Artisti del primo Novecento italiano*, Torino.

1967
- G. Mariacher, *I vetri di Murano*, Milan.

1970
- G. Mariacher, *Il Museo Vetrario di Murano*, Milan.

1972
- M. Brusatin, *Carlo Scarpa*, Monographic issue of Controspazio.
- G. Perocco, *Le origini dell'Arte moderna a Venezia*, Treviso.

1977
- *Vetri di Murano del '900*, Exhibition catalogue, Venice.
- Guido Balsamo Stella, *Opera grafica e vetraria*, Exhibition catalogue, Milan.
- *Carlo Scarpa*, Monographic issue of Space Design.

1978
- S. Tagliapietra, *La magnifica comunità di Murano 1900-1929*, Verona.

1980
- R. Barilli e F. Solmi, *La metafisica: Gli anni Venti*, Bologna.

1981
- *Venezianisches Glas 19 bis 20. Jahrhundert aus dem Glasmuseum Murano/Venezia*, Catalogue, Berlin, Staatliche Museum.
- *Vetri Murano oggi*, Exhibition catalogue, Milan, Electa.
- G. Perocco, *Vittorio Zecchin, etc*; Exhibition catalogue, Venice.
- F. Brunello, *Arti e mestieri a Venezia nel Medioevo e nel Rinascimento*, Neri Pozza.

1982
- R. Barovier Mentasti, *Il vetro veneziano*, Milan, Electa.
- *Mille Anni di arte del vetro a Venezia*, Exhibition catalogue, Venice, Albrizzi.
- S. Tagliapietra, *Cronache muranesi II. Murano veste la divisa 1926-1950*, Venice, Helvetia.
- *Vetro di Murano: ieri ed oggi*, Exhibition catalogue, Tokyo.

1983
- A. Dorigato, *Murano, Il vetro a tavola ieri e oggi*, Exhibition catalogue, Venice.

1984
- F. Dal Co, G.Mazzariol, *Carlo Scarpa 1906-1987*, Milan, Electa.
- M. Miani, D. Resini, F. Lamon, *L'arte dei maestri vetrai di Murano*, Treviso, Matteo.
- *Mostra del vetro italiano 1920-1940*, Exhibition catalogue, Torino, Promark.
- *Venini & the Murano Renaissance*, Exhibition catalogue, New York, Fifty-50.

1985
- *Carlo Scarpa*, Monographic issue of A+U.
- I. De Guitry, M.P. Majno, M. Quesada, *Le arti minori d'autore in Italia dal 1900 al 1970*, Rome.
- A. Dorigato, *Il vetro mosaico muranese*, Bolletino dei Civici musei Veneziani, Venice.
- S. Tagliapietra, *Cronache muranesi: l'Ottocento*, Venice.

1986
- A. Dorigato, *Il Museo Vetrario di Murano*, Milan.

1987
- W. Neuwirth, *Vetri Italiani 1950-1960*, Exhibition catalogue I, Vienna.
- R. Bossaglia, M. Quesada, P. Spadini, *Secessione Romana 1913-1916*, Rome.
- *Gli anni di Cà Pesaro 1908-1920*, Exhibition catalogue, Milan.
- B. Nerozzi, *Impronte del soffio. Tradizioni e nuovi percorsi a Murano*, Exhibition catalogue, Venice.

1988
- *La verrerie Européenne des années 50*. Exhibition catalogue, Marseille, Aveline.
- R. Bossaglia, M. Quesada, *Gabriele D'Annunzio e la promozione delle arti*, Exhibition catalogue, Rome.

1989
- F. Deboni, *I vetri Venini*, Torino, Allemandi.
- *The Venetians, Modern Glass, 1919-1990*. Exhibition catalogue, M. Karasik, New York.
- G. Duplani Tucci, *Venini 1921*, Milano, FMR.
- H. Ricke, *Reflex der Jahrhunderte*, Leipzig, Kunstmuseum Dusseldorf.
- A. Dorigato, *Ercole Barovier 1889-1974, vetraio muranese*, Exhibition catalogue, Venice.
- M. Heiremans, *Murano glass 1945-1970*, Antwerpen.

1990
- *Miniature di vetro, murrine 1838-1924*, Exhibition catalogue, Venice, Arsenale Editrice.

1991
- *Vetri di Murano del '900, 50 capolavori*, Exhibition catalogue, Milan.
- M. Barovier, *Carlo Scarpa. I vetri di Murano 1927-1947*, Venice, Il Cardo.
- U. Franzoi, *I vetri di Archimede Seguso*, Exhibition catalogue, Venice.

1992
- R. Barovier Mentasti, *Vetro Veneziano 1890-1990*, Venice, Arsenale.
- *L'arte del vetro. Silice e fuoco: vetri del XIX e XX secolo*, Exhibition catalogue, Venice, Marsilio.
- M. Barovier, *Napoleone Martinuzzi vetraio del '900*, Exhibition catalogue, Venice, Il Cardo.

1993
- M. Barovier, *L'Arte dei Barovier vetrai di Murano 1866-1972*, Exhibition catalogue, Venice.
- M. Heiremans, *Art Glass from Murano 1910-1970*, Stuttgart, Arnoldsche.
- H. Newman, *Dizionario del vetro*, Milan, Garzanti - Vallardi.
- R. Bossaglia, *I vetri di Fulvio Bianconi*, Exhibition catalogue, Torino.
- S. Lutzeier, *Modernes glas von 1920-1990*, Augsburg.
- L. Pi -a, *Fiftier Glass*, Atglen.

1994
- M. Barovier, *Fantasie di vetro*, Exhibition catalogue, Venice, Arsenale.
- R. Barovier Mentasti, *Vetri veneziani del '900*, Venice, Marsilio.
- G. Sarpellon, *Lino Tagliapietra vetri, glass, verres, glas*, Venice, Arsenale.

1995
- M. Barovier, R. Barovier Mentasti, A. Dorigato, *Il vetro di Murano alle Biennali 1895-1972*, Milan, Leonardo Arte.
- *Glas, Band II*, Zurich, Bellerive Museum.
- R. Barovier Mentasti, *I vetri di Archimede Seguso 1950-1959*, Torino. *La Biennale di Venezia, 46.*
- *Esposizione Internazionale d'Arte*, Catalogue, Venice, Marsilio. H. Ricke, *Glaskunst. Reflex der Jahrhunderte*, Munchen-New York, Prestel.
- *Venezia e la Biennale. I percorsi del gusto*. Exhibition catalogue, Milan, Fabbri.
- *Maestri vetrai creatori di Murano del '900*. Exhibition catalogue, Milan, Electa.
- *L'Art du verre a Murano au 20ème siècle*, Exhibition catalogue, Paris.
- H. Lockwood, *Vetri: Italian Glass News*, April 1995

1996
- M. Barovier, A. Dorigato, *Il bestiario di Murano*, Exhibition catalogue, Venice.
- F. Deboni, *Murano '900*, Milan, Bocca.
- *Gli artisti di Venini. Per una storia del vetro d'arte veneziano*. Exhibition catalogue, Milan, Electa.
- M. Heiremans, *20th century Murano Glass*, Stuttgart, Arnoldsche.
- *Italienisches Glas Murano - Mailand 1930-1970*, Munchen, New York, Prestel.
- *Venezia Aperto Vetro, International New Glass*, Exhibition catalogue, Venice, Arsenale.

1997
- M. Barovier, Carlo Scarpa, *I vetri di un architetto*, Exhibition catalogue, Milan, Skira.
- M. Romanelli, M. Laudani, *Design: Nordest, Milano*, Abitare Segesta.

1998
- M. Barovier, *Tagliapietra, A Venetian Glass Maestro*, Venice, Vitrum (a).
- M. Barovier, B. Bischofberger, M. Carboni, *Sottsass Glass Works*, Venice, Vitrum.
- *Tra creatività e progettazione, il vetro italiano a Milano 1906-1968*, Exhibition catalogue, Milan, Electa.
- *Murrine e Millefiori 1830-1930*, Exhibition catalogue, Venice. Venini Venetian modern glass, Exhibition catalogue, Finland.
- *Venezia Aperto Vetro, International New Glass*, Exhibition catalogue, Venice, Arsenale.
- A. Dorigato, *Vetri veneziani Ohira*, Exhibition catalogue, Venice, Arsenale.
- M. Barovier, *Het Venitiaans glaswerk van Carlo Scarpa*, Exhibition catalogue, Brussels, Skira-Artmedia (b).
- H. Lockwood, *Vetri: Italian Glass News*, Fall 1998

1999
- *Vetri veneziani Ohira 1998-1999*, Exhibition catalogue, Venice, Arsenale.
- Cristiano Bianchin, *Riposapesi*, Exhibition catalogue, Venice.
- M. Barovier, *Il vetro a Venezia, dal moderno al contemporaneo*, Milan, Motta.